CULTURES OF THE WORLD
Bermuda

Cavendish
Square
New York

Published in 2022 by Cavendish Square Publishing, LLC
29 East 21st Street, New York, NY 10010
Copyright © 2022 by Cavendish Square Publishing, LLC

Third Edition

Website: cavendishsq.com

Library of Congress Cataloging-in-Publication Data

Names: Orr, Tamra, author. | Morlock, Rachael, author.
Title: Bermuda / Tamra Orr and Rachael Morlock.
Description: Third edition. | New York : Cavendish Square Publishing,
 [2022] | Series: Cultures of the world | Includes bibliographical
 references and index.
Identifiers: LCCN 2021030977 | ISBN 9781502663009 (library binding) | ISBN
 9781502663016 (ebook)
Subjects: LCSH: Bermuda Islands--Juvenile literature.
Classification: LCC F1631.2 .O77 2022 | DDC 972.99--dc23
LC record available at https://lccn.loc.gov/2021030977

Writers: Tamra B. Orr; Rachael Morlock, third edition
Editor, third edition: Rachael Morlock
Designer, third edition: Jessica Nevins
Picture Researcher, third edition: Jessica Nevins

CPSIA compliance information: Batch #CW22CSQ: For further information contact Cavendish Square Publishing LLC, New York, New York, at 1-877-980-4450.

Printed in the United States of America

CONTENTS

BERMUDA TODAY

A **GENTLY CURVING CRESCENT OF ISLANDS RISES FROM THE SEA** in the western Atlantic Ocean. From a distance, it appears like one formation, but it is really a collection of hundreds of coral islands, cays, and islets. This archipelago, or string of islands, is officially called the Bermuda Islands, though most people know it as Bermuda. Although Bermuda is often thought of as being part of the Caribbean, it is not. It is located far to the north of its Caribbean neighbors. In fact, Bermuda is the most northerly group of coral islands in the world and the only coral atoll in the Atlantic.

PUTTING BERMUDA ON THE MAP

Bermuda is located to the east of the United States and midway between Nova Scotia and the West Indies. It is almost 775 miles (1,247 kilometers) southeast of New York City and 1,030 miles (1,658 km) northeast of Miami, Florida. Bermuda is part of the United Kingdom even though it is located 3,445 miles (5,545 km) away from London, England.

Much of Bermuda is urbanized today, but it still has areas of rich vegetation and diverse wildlife.

Despite this distance, Bermuda is the oldest British territory in the world. Of the many islands and islets that make up its archipelago, 20 are inhabited by people today, but this was not the case more than 500 years ago when European explorers first sighted the islands. At that time, Bermuda was an uninhabited environment occupied mainly by birds and bursting with plant life.

Spanish and Portuguese explorers may have discovered Bermuda first, but it was the English who made it a colony. Bermuda was settled almost by chance when a sinking English ship wrecked on Bermuda's surrounding reefs and its passengers sought refuge on the island. Admiral Sir George Somers, who led the passengers to safety in Bermuda, is still considered a national hero. For a long time, Bermuda was known primarily as the Somers Isles, and the town of St. George is named in Admiral Sir George Somers's honor.

THE EARLY COLONY

When colonists arrived, Bermuda was a densely forested, subtropical ecosystem. Many of the plants and animals that live in Bermuda are unique among the other islands of the Atlantic. Unfortunately, colonial activities diminished the native plant and animal life over the years. However, today, more than 350 bird species can still be spotted in Bermuda. Many are migratory and use Bermuda's environment as a feeding ground during their long journeys north and south. Bermuda's biodiversity also explodes off the coast. There, hundreds of species of coral, fish, marine mammals, sea turtles, and more share the waters surrounding the island.

Bermuda's potential as a maritime base grew alongside its population. The original colony established profitable activities like shipbuilding, salt trading, and agriculture. Its economy grew through the labor of indentured servants and enslaved workers until slavery was abolished in the British territories.

Through the years, Bermuda adapted to the social and economic changes made necessary by war, conflict, and expansion across the Atlantic.

AN ISLAND PARADISE

In the early 20th century, Bermuda realized that one of its greatest economic assets was its natural beauty. Gorgeous scenery, sunny skies, and mild temperatures meant that Bermuda had the makings of an island paradise. The country marketed this beauty, and soon travelers were arriving from around the world. Tourism was the main economic industry for most of the 1900s. At the end of the century, Bermuda seized a new opportunity in international business. This shift is responsible for the economic prosperity now enjoyed in Bermuda. Tourism and international business together have made Bermuda a high-income country today.

Bermuda is still a major tourist destination, especially for travelers from North America. Pink sand beaches and adventurous activities like snorkeling, scuba diving, and deep-sea fishing are famous attractions. Bermuda is the perfect place for those looking for a taste of British culture outside of Great Britain. In addition, there are colorful festivals, delicious foods, and a population of people with diverse cultural and ethnic backgrounds. Bermuda has been a favorite spot for artists and writers inspired by the enviornment.

Of course, Bermuda is not always a paradise. The country has a complex history, steeped in everything from rum-running and piracy to espionage and racial strife. Racial inequalities are rooted in the island's history of slavery and discrimination. Pressure for change reached a tipping point through organized protests, demonstrations, and riots in the second half of the 20th century. They ushered in major reforms in Bermuda's government and society, but the struggle for equity continues today.

Some of the biggest hurdles facing modern-day Bermuda have to do with global climate change and the pressures of a large population on a small stretch of land. Fortunately, Bermuda's government not only cares about its fragile environment, but it is also willing to spend money and time to protect it. It is unclear what other challenges lie ahead, but Bermudians have resources, resilience, and inventiveness on their side.

GEOGRAPHY

An aerial view of Bermuda shows the archipelago's curving shape surrounded by reefs.

1

"These leafy isles
upon the ocean
thrown,
Like studs of
emerald o'er a silver
zone."
—Thomas Moore,
1804

BERMUDA IS AN ARCHIPELAGO THAT forms a fishhook shape in the Atlantic Ocean. The string of islands is 24 miles (40 km) long, and on average less than 1 mile (1.6 km) wide. The nearest landmass is Cape Hatteras, North Carolina, which is about 670 miles (1,078 km) to the west.

The archipelago is built on a base of volcanic rock. Historians believe the volcano crested above the sea more than 100 million years ago and erupted about 34 million years ago. Bermuda was surrounded by reefs, most of which are still underwater today. Over time, constant winds and water carried limestone deposits across the ocean. Eventually, the islands formed a limestone layer roughly 300 feet (91 meters) thick with a top layer of fertile soil. There are no natural lakes or rivers in Bermuda, and rain is the only reliable source of fresh water.

Bermuda's archipelago is made up of 138 islands and countless small islets, rocks, and caves. About 170 of these landmasses are named and recorded, but there are close to 300 altogether. Although Bermuda is actually made of many landforms, it is usually referred to singularly as an island.

MAIN ISLANDS

The largest islands are Great Bermuda (or Main Island); St. George's and St. David's in the east; and Somerset, Watford, Boaz, and Ireland in the west. They vary in size but are all connected by a series of bridges. Great Bermuda makes up more than 14 miles (22.5 km) of the archipelago's length. It is small enough that you can cross from the east side to the west side in only an hour on foot. If you want to travel by car from the north side to the south side, it will only take about 15 minutes. The islands are mildly hilly and mostly low. The highest elevation is 259 feet (79 m) and is located on the Main Island.

DIVIDING THE ISLANDS

The inhabited islands of Bermuda are divided into nine parishes: Devonshire, Hamilton, Paget, Pembroke, Sandys, Smith's, Southampton, St. George's, and Warwick. Originally known as the tribes, Bermuda's parishes were named after stockholders in the Somers Island Company. The company was appointed by England's King James in 1615 to operate the island colony. These stockholders were mainly aristocrats who never or rarely visited Bermuda.

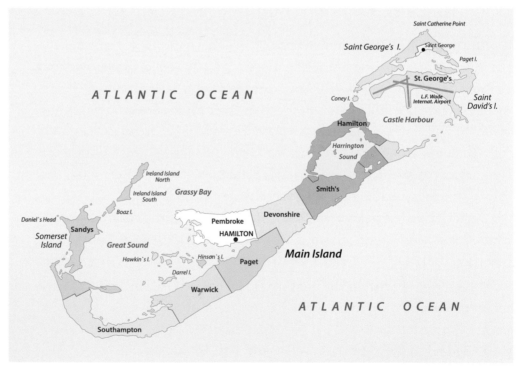

This map shows the division of Bermuda into nine parishes. The names have been unchanged since 1620.

AN UNEXPECTED DISCOVERY

In 1907, two young boys named Carl Gibbons and Edgar Hollis were playing cricket. A strong hit sent the ball rolling away. Suddenly, it disappeared down a mysterious hole.

Following the ball, the two boys discovered some unbelievably huge and intricate underground limestone caves. Shaped like a Gothic cathedral, these "Crystal Caves," so called for the clear water inside them, are now a favorite tourist attraction in Bermuda. There are more than 150 limestone caves scattered throughout Bermuda, many of them reaching deep below sea level. Experts believe many of the caves date back to the Ice Age. Exploration in these caves has resulted in the discovery of 75 water and cave-adapted species, including worms, mites, and crustaceans.

The Crystal Caves are a major tourist attraction for visitors interested in a close look at the stalactites and stalagmites that have formed over centuries.

Each parish is roughly the same size: about 2.3055 square miles (6 square kilometers). There are no signs on the island to indicate when you pass out of one parish into another. Although they are very similar, there are a few differences in how developed each area is and how many people choose to live in each parish.

St. George's Parish at the eastern tip includes the town of St. George, the second English colony to be settled after Jamestown, Virginia. The town was Bermuda's capital until 1815. It has streets with old-fashioned, quaint names like Old Maid's Lane, Petticoat Alley, and Thread and Needle Alley. It also has a section known as Tucker's Town—the least populated inhabited area on the entire archipelago—which is inhabited only by the exceptionally wealthy.

Hamilton Parish is home to extensive cave systems, along with the Bermuda Aquarium, Museum, and Zoo. Smith's Parish is the top choice for hikers and those who love soaking in the scenery because it features multiple nature and wildlife reserves. The reef at John Smith's Bay Park and Beach is a favorite spot for visitors to see hundreds of colorful fish. It also features the Portuguese Rock, a stone with markings on it dating back to 1543.

Devonshire Parish is full of rolling hills and nature preserves perfect for a day of bird watching. Pembroke Parish is the home of the City of Hamilton, Bermuda's capital, and is full of government buildings. Paget Parish is the best place to see many types of migratory birds or for tourists to spend time and money in the area's luxury resorts.

Warwick Parish is a dream come true for either golfers or horseback riders, while Southampton Parish has Horseshoe Bay, Bermuda's most famous beach. Sandys Parish, at the very tip of the Main Island, features the Gilbert Nature Reserve and the Royal Naval Dockyard, also known as the Gibraltar of the West, similar to the British territory in the Strait of Gibraltar. Built in 1809, the dockyard once housed convicts from Britain and Bermuda. Today, it is a tourist center and a popular stop for families on vacation.

BIRDS AND WILDLIFE

Bermuda is full of fascinating creatures, from those overhead to those on land and in the waters. The island has more than 1,600 species of plants and animals. Only a quarter of them are actually native to the islands. Three-quarters of the species were intentionally brought over or arrived accidentally as stowaways on plants or in cargo. Butterflies, caterpillars, spiders, bees, snails, cats, dogs, cattle, chickens, and horses were transported to the island by humans.

If there is any creature that represents the sound of Bermuda, it is the whistling frog. This tiny tree frog first arrived on the island on imported plants in the 1880s. The nocturnal amphibian is incredibly small—one could fit on the average person's thumbnail. During the day, these brown frogs hide under leaves and stones. As soon as night falls, they climb up into the trees, thanks to special suction-like padding on their long, thin toes. Those pads make them good climbers but terrible swimmers since they have no webbing between their toes. Once in the trees, male frogs begin to chirp or sing. The song is the way the males attract female frogs. Their songs fill the night air from April through November. Tourists sometimes struggle to get used to the noise, but it is one that Bermudians love.

The island is also home to giant toads, which are also called marine toads. They were imported from Guyana in 1885 to control insects. The giant toads prey on garden insects, cockroaches, centipedes, lizards, frogs, mice, and younger toads. They have a set of poison glands that emit a toxin, or poisonous substance, that can be harmful to predators (and dogs). The female giant toad's eggs are poisonous also. Drawn to the warmth of the road at day's end, these hand-sized toads often get run over by night traffic.

Bermuda is also home to a variety of lizards, from the black rock lizard known as the Bermuda skink to the Somerset lizard with an eye patch that makes it look like a bandit. Fossilized skink bones have been found in limestone caves dating back 300,000 years. The 8-inch (20 centimeter) Bermuda skink is the only land vertebrate to have lived on Bermuda since before the first humans arrived.

Birds of all kinds fill the skies over these islands. Over 200 migrating species nest in the area between Christmas and Easter, and about two dozen stay year-round. The cahow, or Bermuda petrel, does not live in the trees of Bermuda but instead burrows in the sand in some of the isolated eastern islands. These seabirds can both fly and float in the water. They are so elusive that experts thought they were long extinct until the 1950s. Other species found throughout the island include eastern warblers, martins, doves, terns, egrets, and herons. Many of these were introduced by humans, including the kiskadee, a bird brought in to help control the island's lizards and flies. It ate many of those pests—but now, it is a pest to fruit crops and native species.

There are huge numbers of insects in Bermuda because of the island's consistently warm and wet climate. Mosquitoes are prevalent, as are

The scarlet ibis is a colorful presence in Bermuda. It uses its long, hooked bill to forage for carotene-rich crustaceans in shallow water or mud.

grasshoppers, moths, fleas, and three types of wasps, including the red bee, which can sting multiple times.

SEA LIFE

There are more than 600 species of fish in the waters off Bermuda and about 30 different coral species. Castle Harbour and St. George's Harbour, as well as Harrington Sound and Great Sound, are home to an interesting array of creatures. They include black fin tuna, marlin, wahoo, swordfish, dolphin, and barracuda. Visitors who walk the beaches often find hundreds of oval chitons, a type of mollusk that clings to the rocks and is known locally as a suck-rock.

Sharks are fairly prevalent in the ocean around Bermuda too. Most of the types found here, usually Galapagos and dusky sharks, are harmless and rarely come close to the shore. One of the most dangerous nearby creatures is the Portuguese man-of-war. It lives in the water year-round but is known to wash up on shore between March and July, especially after tropical storms. These creatures are often huge, with tentacles reaching up to 165 feet (50 m) long. The long tentacles can sting with about 75 percent of the toxicity of a

Pink sand beaches are Bermuda's claim to fame as a result of foraminifera.

ENDEMIC SPECIES

An endemic species is one that comes to a place naturally and then evolves into a unique form that is not found anywhere else. A clue that a species is endemic here is the addition of "Bermuda" to its name. That means that the species is only found on this unique archipelago.

Bermuda's endemic plant species include trees like the Bermuda cedar, Bermuda palmetto, and Bermuda olivewood. Forest floors used to be covered with species such as Bermuda sedge, the moss Bermuda trichostoma, Bermuda maidenhair fern, and the shrub Bermuda snowberry. Flowers like the Bermudiana still bloom on the island, and nature lovers may come across the Bermuda buckeye butterfly, the archipelago's only endemic butterfly. The Bermuda skink is the islands' historic lizard resident. The Bermuda petrel is more commonly known as the cahow. Since the 1950s, it has made a miraculous recovery from near extinction thanks to dedicated conservation projects.

cobra. This man-of-war species should be avoided; even when it looks dead on the sand, it can still sting.

One of Bermuda's smallest creatures is also one of its most influential because it creates the country's famous pink beaches. A single-celled animal, the foraminifer lives on the bottom of the reefs. It has a bright pink skeleton with holes throughout. It sticks feet-like roots out of those holes and uses them to cling to the reef. When it dies, its skeleton separates from its roots and floats up onto the shore. There, it is ground up into tiny pieces by the pounding surf and creates the unique pink sand found on the island's beaches.

The ocean around Bermuda is also a sanctuary for whales, including the northern and humpback varieties. In the winter months, these whales swim to warm waters to mate and give birth. The trip is up to 4,000 miles (6,437 km) each way, one of the longest in the entire animal kingdom. Part of the journey takes them right past Bermuda in March and April. They stop by to eat their favorite food, krill, which until recently scientists did not think existed in Bermuda. Krill are small crustaceans—creatures with hard exoskeletons, jointed legs, and segmented bodies. They gather together in groups and are a whale's favorite snack.

Hibiscus flowers thrive in Bermuda's subtropical climate.

Two other unusual creatures on the islands are the rare Bermuda land crab, which can sometimes grow up to a foot wide, and the Bermuda fireworm, a glow worm that shines in shallow waters. The fireworm mates from May to October on the third night after a full moon, exactly 56 minutes after sunset. The female worm comes to the water's surface, and chemicals make her glow as she swims in circles. This attracts the male, who swims up to join the dance. As the worms' eggs and sperm mix, there is a brilliant green flash. It lasts only a few seconds and then disappears. A month later, when the full moon returns, so do the fireworms and their unearthly light.

FLORA

Growing plants and flowers in Bermuda is a balancing act. On the one hand, the weather is perfect. There is a lot of sun and warmth year-round to help vegetation grow, and the soil is relatively fertile. On the other hand, rain is far from predictable. Unlike many islands, Bermuda does not have an official rainy season. Rainfall in Bermuda averages about 5 inches (127 millimeters) per month. Fresh water is in short supply throughout Bermuda, so when rain falls, it is typically used for drinking and cooking rather than watering plants.

Nonetheless, some plants and flowers do manage to survive and even thrive on these islands. The cassava plant has tuberlike roots and is often ground into flour and used in dishes like Christmas pies. Other plants include the prickly pear, yucca, and banana. The only endemic palm on the island is the Bermuda palmetto. In the past, settlers used the large leaves to make thatched roofs. They also crushed and fermented the fronds to make a strong alcohol called bibby. Parts of the plants were even used to fashion women's hats during the 1600s. Other trees include pine, casuarina, mangrove, and a growing number of cedars. Mangrove forests are unique this far north in the

Atlantic, but the warming Gulf Stream makes their growth possible. Flowers such as oleander, poinsettia, Easter lily, hibiscus, bougainvillea, Bermudiana, and three species of morning glory can be found in Bermuda.

The one plant that truly symbolizes Bermuda, however, is the onion. Originally introduced in 1616 from England, it grew fantastically well in the island soil. In the 19th century, it became an export crop to many places, including the United States. The vegetable became so popular and successful for Bermuda that Bermudians are often referred to as "Onions." It is a nickname that is still heard on the islands today.

Two of the best places to see and appreciate the beauty of Bermuda's flora are the Palm Grove Gardens and the Bermuda Botanical Gardens. Palm Grove is located on a private estate that is open to the public. It features a lily pond depicting the entire Bermuda archipelago as a living map. The Botanical Gardens cover 36 acres (14.5 hectares) where visitors can wander through a maze, a sensory garden, and a display of Bermuda's native species.

CLIMATE

One of the most alluring aspects of Bermuda, of course, is its warm and subtropical climate. Snow is unheard of here, and even cloudy days are rare. Between May and October, the average daily temperature ranges between 75 and 85 degrees Fahrenheit (24 and 29 degrees Celsius). Even during the cooler season, from December through March, the average temperature does not go below 60°F (15°C). Though Bermuda does not have an official rainy season, most of the year it is quite humid, making a swim in the sound or ocean a welcome treat. When it does rain, it tends to be a sudden, short downpour rather than a drizzle that can last for several hours. The average rainfall in one year is 57 inches (145 cm).

While many ocean islands worry about regular and devastating hurricanes, Bermuda is less affected. Hurricanes and tropical storms are a problem, but they tend to blow by rather than strike head-on due to the island's geographic location. The worst hurricane to hit Bermuda in recent history was Hurricane Fabian in 2003.

SPITTAL POND NATURE RESERVE

Many call Spittal Pond Nature Reserve in Smith's Parish—with its rocky shores, salt marsh habitat, mudland flats, and leafy trails—the most beautiful place in Bermuda. It is Bermuda's largest nature reserve, spanning 64 acres (26 ha). About 20 bird species live in the wetland habitat, including waterfowl like herons, sandpipers, and egrets. More than 200 other bird species feed in the area during their yearly migration. Visitors might also catch a glimpse of two of Bermuda's endemic species: the Bermuda buckeye butterfly or the Bermuda skink.

The main pond at the reserve contains brackish water. Fresh water turns brackish when storms or floods send salt water into the pond. Black mangroves grow along the main pond, thriving in this habitat. A geological formation known as the Checkerboard is also part of the reserve. The pressures of plate tectonics have resulted in a checkerboard of fractured limestone.

THE BERMUDA TRIANGLE

Even if you are unfamiliar with Bermuda, you have likely heard of the Bermuda Triangle. The Bermuda or Devil's Triangle really has little to do with Bermuda at all—it is just the name for a triangular area of ocean between Bermuda, Puerto Rico, and Florida. The Bermuda Triangle has become the source of endless legends and stories about disappearing ships, airplanes, and people. Books have been written and movies filmed that imply this 440,000—square mile (1,140,000 sq km) area is a source of some kind of supernatural power.

Supposedly, the triangle's power was known all the way back in Christopher Columbus's time. Legend states that while sailing through this part of the ocean, all of his ships' compasses began spinning and sailors saw strange lights in the sky.

In March 1918, the USS *Cyclops* and its entire crew were lost at sea in this area and never found again. In December 1945, five U.S. bomber planes disappeared in this area, as well as the seaplane that went looking for them. No bodies or wreckage were ever recovered.

Over the years, there have been more than 200 such incidents reported in this area. Although some are sure that the Bermuda Triangle is a dangerous and mysterious place, many experts have shown how each incident occurred—scientifically. Usually, their theories involve violent storms, downward air currents, and simple logic. Other plausible theories include waterspouts, underwater earthquakes, and even attacks by modern-day pirates.

When the U.S. Board on Geographic Names was barraged by messages from travelers who were worried about the so-called Bermuda Triangle, it decided it was time to make an official statement. "We do not recognize the Bermuda Triangle as an official name and do not maintain an official file on the area," it stated. "The 'Bermuda' or 'Devil's Triangle' is an imaginary area located off the southeastern Atlantic coast of the United States, which is noted for a high incidence of unexplained losses of ships, small boats, and aircraft. The apexes of the triangle are generally accepted to be Bermuda, Miami, and San Juan. In the past, extensive but futile Coast Guard searches prompted by search and rescue cases such as the disappearances of an entire squadron of TBM Avengers shortly after take off from Fort Lauderdale, or the traceless sinking of *Marine Sulphur Queen* in the Florida Straits, have lent credence to the popular belief in the mystery and the supernatural qualities of the Bermuda Triangle."

INTERNET LINKS

bamz.org
The Bermuda Zoological Society supports the work of the Bermuda Aquarium, Museum, and Zoo in educating people about Bermuda's diverse animal life.

environment.bm
The Government of Bermuda's Department of Environment and Natural Resources offers links with information about biodiversity, habitats, and species in Bermuda.

www.audubon.bm
Visit the website of the Bermuda Audubon Society and learn about Bermuda's efforts to conserve special birdlife.

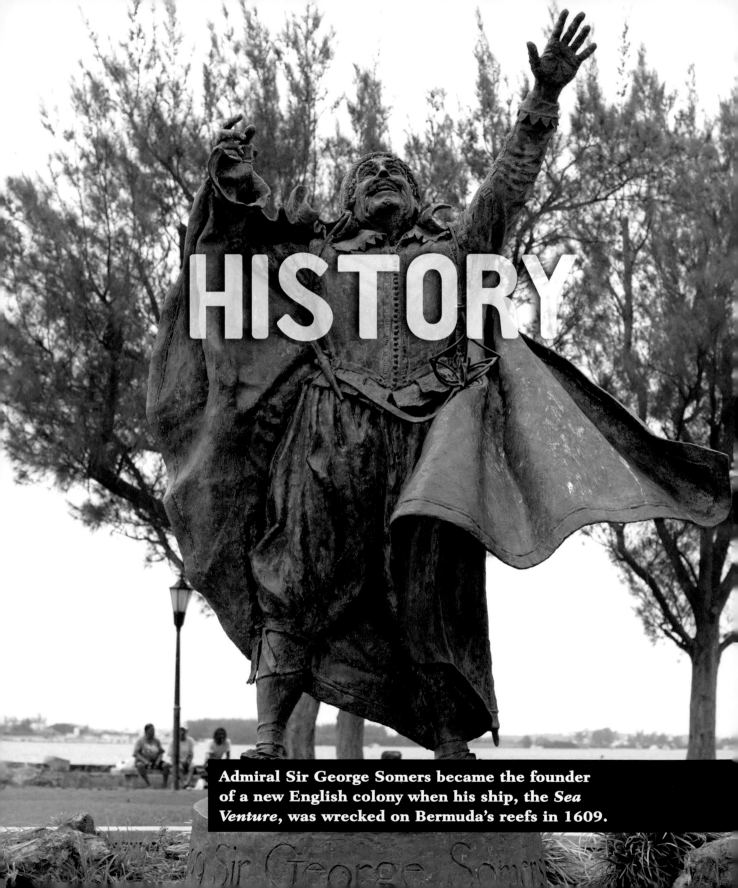

HISTORY

Admiral Sir George Somers became the founder of a new English colony when his ship, the *Sea Venture*, was wrecked on Bermuda's reefs in 1609.

2

THE AGE OF EXPLORATION SWEPT across the world from the 15th through 17th centuries. European sailors ventured out into the unknown with the help of new technologies. They documented and changed the unmapped world as they found it. Until the 16th century, the uninhabited islands of Bermuda were a mystery. As Spanish and Portuguese ships crossed the Atlantic Ocean with greater regularity, Bermuda began to slowly emerge from the shadows. Explorers and shipwrecked sailors alike increased the world's knowledge of the archipelago through each encounter with the island. Over 100 years passed between the discovery of Bermuda and its settlement by humans. In the following 400 years, Bermuda became an important British colony with its own complex history of growth and change.

"I sayled (sailed) above the island Bermuda, otherwise called Garza, being the furthest of all islands that are found at this day in the world."

—Gonzalo Fernández de Oviedo, 1515

One of the earliest landings in Bermuda was recorded in a cliffside rock carving. The inscription includes the year 1543, two initials, and a cross. The initials have been interpreted as "R. P." and likely stand for the Latin words "Rex Portugaliae," or "King of Portugal." The cross resembles that of the Portuguese Order of Christ.

Historians believe the rock was carved by sailors from a Portuguese slave ship that crashed on the nearby reefs. Survivors lived on the island while they constructed a small, seaworthy vessel made from salvaged ship materials and turtle shells. After leaving their mark on Bermuda, the remaining crew sailed for Puerto Rico.

The landmark was long called Spanish Rock due to a misunderstanding of its inscription. It was renamed Portuguese Rock in 2009. Although the original rock is no longer in place, a bronze cast of the inscription can be visited in Spittal Pond.

EXPLORERS AND SEAFARERS

As early as 1503, a Spanish explorer named Juan de Bermúdez is thought to have sailed by what is now the Bermuda archipelago. He saw the beauty of the island, but probably only from afar. The treacherous reefs surrounding Bermuda were far too menacing for him to dock on his initial trip. He returned to Spain full of stories of the wonders he had seen. By 1511, the island was being added to maps, and it was named after the first man to note its existence. Gonzalo Fernández de Oviedo sailed near the archipelago in 1515 and recognized the place named for Bermúdez.

Further reports about the island made their way back to Europe, and interest in Bermuda began to increase. Captain Bartolomé Carreño spent 25 days on the island in 1538. His survey, describing the features, resources, possible ports, and potential value of Bermuda, was sent to Spain along with a shipment of cedar from the island.

In 1603, Captain Diego Ramirez and his Spanish ship ran aground in the area during a storm. The crew spent several weeks in Bermuda repairing their ship. During this time, Ramirez sent a man named Venturilla to row ashore and gather cedar wood. Venturilla is believed to be the first Black man to land on Bermuda. He approached the island alone at night with a lantern and an axe for chopping wood. The light of his lantern sparked a scuffle with a group of surprised cahows, Bermuda's native seabird. Venturilla was alarmed by the birds' loud, harsh cries, and the ship's crew came to his aid. Ramirez later recorded that the crew captured and clubbed more than 500 birds that night, which they then used for food. When they returned to Spain, Ramirez wrote reports about the island resources and wildlife he encountered and created maps to help guide others across the ocean to the archipelago.

FIRST INHABITANTS

When the *Sea Venture* set sail from Plymouth, England, in July 1609, it carried passengers on their way to new lives in the Jamestown colony of Virginia. Led by Admiral Sir George Somers, they ran into trouble before reaching Virginia. A violent storm developed and blew the sinking ship off course and directly into the reefs around Bermuda's islands. The 150 passengers fought their way through the water and made it to shore. They were stranded on the island for

A replica of the *Deliverance*, the ship built in 1609 by the shipwrecked *Sea Venture* passengers, can be visited in St. George's, Bermuda.

10 months and spent most of the time building two ships called *Patience* and *Deliverance*. All but two of the survivors got on the new ships headed to Virginia in May 1610. Christopher Carter and Robert Waters (and later Edward Chard) stayed behind and became Bermuda's first permanent settlers. Somers soon returned to the island to gather more food and provisions for Jamestown, but he died there on November 9, 1610. His heart was buried in Bermuda according to his wishes.

That same year, King James I of England gave Bermuda to the Virginia Company, a corporation charged with the settlement of Virginia. About 60 British settlers sailed on *The Plough* to the islands to start a colony in 1612. They were led by Richard Moore, who acted as the group's first governor. A mere two years later, the Virginia Company gave Bermuda back to England because stockholders lost interest. Profits were slim, settlers had died of disease and starvation, and too many ships were wrecked to make the venture worthwhile.

ESTABLISHING THE COLONY

King James placed Bermuda in the hands of the Somers Island Company, or Bermuda Company, in 1615. The first Bermuda parliament convened in 1620, and soon the State House was built to accommodate future meetings. Because it was so far away from England, Bermuda remained an outpost operated by the Somers Island Company. It was a self-governing entity divided into tribes until the company dissolved in 1684. Bermuda was then named an official British Crown Colony under King Charles II. Its tribes became known as parishes.

The population of the island expanded as indentured servants and enslaved laborers were brought to Bermuda. Indentured servants were usually poor, young white men from the British Isles. They agreed to work for a certain period, usually seven years, in exchange for their passage to Bermuda. At the end of their service, indentured servants were released and given tools and two suits of clothing to set up their new life in Bermuda. Prisoners from Scotland and Ireland were sold into a life of servitude in Bermuda as well.

In the earliest years of the colony, Black people primarily came to Bermuda as indentured servants. In fact, Bermuda was the first British colony to use Black indentured servants. The first known case of enslavement occurred in

1616, when Governor Daniel Tucker brought an enslaved Native American and an enslaved African man to the islands as divers. Pearl diving was not a success in Bermuda, but slavery became increasingly common as the transatlantic slave trade grew and the need for labor on the islands increased. Enslaved laborers were brought to Bermuda from the West Indies or taken from Spanish and Portuguese ships.

Native Americans from New England were sold into slavery in Bermuda as war captives. After the 1637 Pequot War in Massachusetts, at least 80 Pequot people were taken to Bermuda. The end of King Philip's War, another conflict between New England colonists and indigenous people, also led to the transport of a large group of war captives to Bermuda in the 1670s. Many of the Native Americans sold into slavery in Bermuda were Pequots, Wampanoags, Narragansetts, Cherokees, Mohegans, Carib, Arowacks, and Central and South American Indians.

Bermuda's economy grew, bolstered by the system of slave labor. As the global slave trade expanded, white attitudes toward Black Bermudians became more hostile. A set of 1622 laws restricted the economic activities of Black Bermudians. Throughout the years of slavery, there were some Black Bermudians who maintained their freedom. However, changing attitudes and the ramped up slave trade significantly lowered their political and social status. Some Black indentured servants were forced or sold into slavery despite their original contracts. Enslaved Black or Native American people could be sold and then put to work as house servants, field workers, boatmen, fishermen, crew men at ports, shipwrights, shoemakers, masons, carpenters, or other laborers.

Bermuda experimented with agricultural crops, including sugarcane and tobacco, which could be exported to England. However, the soil was not fertile enough for these crops to thrive, and they were abandoned by the mid-17th century. Instead, most colonists and enslaved workers focused on building ships using the plentiful resource of cedar on the island. The Bermuda sloop became a major product.

Trade by sea was also an important element of life in Bermuda. A vital trade was established in the 1660s when Bermudians began producing salt on the uninhabited Turks Islands. Salt was essential for preserving food, and exporting this "white gold" to the American colonies was extremely profitable.

One-tenth of Bermudians made their living through the salt trade in the 1750s.

By the 1750s, Bermudians were trading as much as 130,000 bushels of salt every year. The salt trade led to friction and near war between Bermuda and the Bahamas in the 1770s when the Bahamas sought control of the Turks Islands. Power over the Turks Islands and the regulation of their rewarding salt pans was formally granted to the Bahamas in 1803. Bermudians were able to continue the trade by paying taxes to the Bahamas.

COLONIAL CHALLENGES

Challenges to the trading partnership between Bermuda and the American colonies were posed by the American Revolution (1775—1783). Bermuda officially maintained its loyalty to Great Britain throughout the war. As a result, a number of American colonies cut off trading with Bermuda. This created a hardship since the people of Bermuda depended on America for food and other supplies. Many Bermudians had to find another way to get the goods and supplies they needed. Some turned to piracy, attacking ships for whatever supplies they could possibly steal. Others continued to trade illegally with the colonies. Bermudians also began tearing down and salvaging whatever they could from the ships that had wrecked on their shores.

Despite its official Loyalist stance, public opinion about the American Revolution was divided in Bermuda. Trade restrictions brought some islanders close to starvation. Soon, the government was compelled to propose a deal with the American Continental Congress.

In 1775, Colonel Henry Tucker traveled to Philadelphia, Pennsylvania, to offer a trade of salt for grain. The Congress suggested that, although they were not interested in salt, a shipload of British gunpowder would secure an equal exchange of food. Several weeks later, 100 barrels of gunpowder from the British magazine in St. George's were secretly loaded onto boats bound for American ports. The embargo on trade with Bermuda was lifted in response, and the food and salt trade resumed between the Atlantic neighbors. After the war ended, Bermuda began to thrive once again. It set up a healthy merchant trade system with the West Indies and the North American continent.

Bermuda became an even more crucial British outpost after the American Revolution. Important American ports had been lost, and the British needed

A LETTER FROM GEORGE WASHINGTON

George Washington sent his own request for gunpowder to Bermuda on September 6, 1775: "We are informed there is a very large Magazine in your Island under a very feeble Guard [...] We knew not therefore to what Extent to sollicit your Assistance in availing ourselves of this Supply;—but if your Favor and Friendship to North America and its Liberties have not been misrepresented, I persuade myself you may, consistent with your own Safety, pro mote and further this Scheme, so as to give it the fairest prospect of Success. Be assured, that in this Case, the whole Power and Execution of my Influence will be made with the Honble. Continental Congress, that your Island may not only be Supplied with Provisions, but experience every other Mark of Affection and Friendship, which the grateful Citizens of a free Country can bestow on its Brethren and Benefactors."

to establish a new mid-Atlantic base. In 1809, construction of the Royal Naval Dockyards began in Bermuda through the labor of enslaved workers and convicts. The dockyard and port were built across 200 acres (80 ha) of Ireland Island and became one of the largest maritime bases in the 19th century.

The stronghold was ready for action by the time the next conflict erupted—the War of 1812. The position of the dockyards as the hub of the Royal Navy made a blockade of American ports possible. In 1814, ships carrying more than 5,000 British troops sailed out of the Bermuda docks to bombard Baltimore, Maryland; and Washington, D.C. The troops were successful in setting fire to the White House, and their capture of Francis Scott Key in Baltimore inspired him to write the song that later became the U.S. national anthem.

EMANCIPATION

Besides being frequently caught in the middle of larger world conflicts, Bermuda had its own, more immediate challenges. The institution of slavery was one of the largest problems on the island, and it was a source of political and social unrest. Several revolts were organized in Bermuda in the 17th and 18th centuries, but they were all unsuccessful in bringing about a change for enslaved Bermudians.

In 1807, the slave trade was outlawed in the British Empire. Although enslaved people could no longer be legally bought or sold in the outposts of the British Empire, slavery itself continued. In British colonies like Bermuda, those who were already enslaved remained enslaved.

Mary Prince was an enslaved woman who was born in Bermuda. In 1828, she traveled with her enslaver's family from the British colony of Antigua to England. Slavery was illegal in England at the time, so Prince left her enslaver's home and made a bid for freedom to the British government. She became the first person to present an antislavery petition to Parliament in London. Though Prince was free on English soil, she was not able to return to her husband in Antigua or she could be enslaved again. Prince stayed in England, where she published her life story in 1831. The experiences of brutality and pain she described shocked readers. Her autobiography helped the antislavery movement in the United Kingdom.

Through the efforts of Prince and other antislavery activists, the Emancipation Act was passed by Parliament in 1833. This act required the end of slavery and the emancipation of all enslaved people in the British colonies. The major change was scheduled to take effect in 1834.

As Bermuda prepared to end slavery, a flurry of activity occurred in anticipation of the social changes. Formerly enslaved people would be free, but they would not be politically equal to their peers. Laws were introduced with property requirements for voting in elections, serving on juries, or running for Parliament. These laws were intended to restrict the activities of newly freed people, and there was a notable absence of legislation that would help them establish an economically independent status.

Where Bermuda's government failed to provide support, local groups stepped in with vital resources and assistance. These groups were called Friendly Societies, and they played a crucial role after emancipation. Societies and lodges offered financial help for members of their community who were struggling. Joseph Henry Thomas, a free Black man, was a leading force in establishing Friendly Societies and organizing education for freed Black Bermudians. He helped found lodges in St. George's, Hamilton, and Sandys

Mary Prince published her autobiography, The History of Mary Prince: A West Indian Slave Narrative, *in 1831. She was the first Black woman to publish a book in Britain. In it, Prince wrote: "Oh the horrors of slavery!—How the thought of it pains my heart! But the truth ought to be told of it; and what my eyes have seen I think it is my duty to relate; for few people in England know what slavery is. I have been a slave—I have felt what a slave feels, and I know what a slave knows; and I would have all the good people in England to know it too, that they break our chains, and set us free."*

that are still functional today. In 1846, Thomas became headmaster of the Lane School, which was one of Bermuda's first schools for free Black residents.

Even after emancipation, Black Bermudians did not have equal rights. Schools and public places were segregated, and employment opportunities were limited. Furthermore, the economic disadvantages related to a history of slavery prevented Black Bermudians from participation or representation in Bermuda's government.

WAR AND CHANGE

When the American Civil War (1861—1865) began in the United States, Bermuda helped the pro-slavery South. Blockade-runners from Bermuda carried essential exports to the South. Large ships from the United Kingdom were also allowed to unload cargoes of arms and ammunition, cannons, gunpowder, lead, and other weapons on the islands. The supplies were stored in warehouses in Bermuda until they could be loaded onto ships headed for the Confederate states. This brought much-needed money to the islanders, as Southern leaders paid huge sums to rent Bermuda's warehouses and wharves. St. George's Harbour became the base for smuggling manufactured goods from the United Kingdom into the Confederate ports.

When the Confederacy fell and the South lost the war, Bermuda had to search for another source of income once again. This time it turned to

Fort St. Catherine was constructed in 1614 to protect against attacks by sea. It is Bermuda's largest fort.

agriculture. To help with the growth of vegetables such as celery, potatoes, tomatoes, and onions, Bermuda brought in emigrants from Portugal.

International wars and events continued to influence the growth of Bermuda in the 20th century. A U.S. naval base was built on the island during World War I (1914—1918), bringing in more people and more jobs. Quite a few Bermudians signed up for service overseas in the segregated Black Bermuda Militia Artillery and white Bermuda Volunteer Rifle Corps.

During Prohibition (1919—1933) in the United States, Bermuda forged another key relationship. Prohibition resulted from the passage of 18th Amendment to the U.S. Constitution in 1919, which stated that making, selling, or transporting alcohol was illegal throughout the United States. Alcohol, especially Bermuda's famous rum, was smuggled into the country in a process referred to as rum-running. Alcohol from Europe was also shipped to a depot in Bermuda where it could be stored before delivery to "rum-row," a strip of international water where smugglers could unload just offshore of the United States and outside its legal power.

Bermuda's involvement in World War II (1939–1945) was much more expansive than in previous wars. In fact, Bermuda became an underground source for some of the most important espionage in the world. Underneath the Hamilton Princess Hotel, a trained staff of young men and women worked around the clock to decode the radio signals going to and from German submarines and other vessels in the Atlantic. They were able to break the Nazi code and let the Allies know what the Germans were planning. Once the United States entered the war, FBI agents joined British spies in Bermuda and helped them crack more codes.

During the war, Bermuda was also a refueling stop for airplanes flying between Europe and the United States. While there, the pilots would rest. This gave British and Bermudian spies the chance to sneak onto the airplanes and read the mail onboard. Many times, secret messages were sent using invisible ink, and they would be deciphered and passed on. The people who were especially skilled at opening sealed envelopes, reading what was inside, and resealing the envelopes were known as trappers. Most of the time they were young women.

Bermudian spies also realized that the Germans had found a new way to send important messages back and forth. They were able to shrink a regular page of type down to the size of a dot and then hide it in a message under a period or other form of punctuation. The hidden text could be anywhere in the letter. They said their search for the hidden text was like finding raisins scattered throughout a bowl of pudding known as plum duff. This top-secret method for uncovering messages was nicknamed the duff method.

At the start of World War II, English prime minister Winston Churchill offered to lease part of Bermuda to President Franklin D. Roosevelt if the United States would help them fight the Germans. Roosevelt agreed, and Bermuda leased a rent-free portion of land to the United States to build military bases.

A U.S. Navy station for seaplanes and a U.S. Army airfield opened in 1941. U.S. service members and their families became fixtures in Bermuda until 1995 when the 99-year lease ended early and the land was returned to Bermuda.

Bermuda's central location had often been used in the midst of conflict throughout its history. However, after World War II, Bermuda became a unifying meeting ground, especially for the United Kingdom and the United States. A period of diplomatic meetings on the island between world powers began with a famous 1953 summit. The "Big Three" conference brought together British prime minister Winston Churchill, U.S. president Dwight D. Eisenhower, and French prime minister Joseph Laniel.

DESEGREGATION AND EQUALITY

Even as international conflicts were resolved, internal problems were brewing in Bermuda's postwar years. Racial segregation in schools, hotels, restaurants, theaters, sports clubs, and other public places like banks and offices was the norm in Bermuda. Many argued that segregation was necessary for maintaining U.S. tourism. Property restrictions for voting, serving on juries, or holding office still prevented many Black citizens from having a voice in their government. Racial tensions were worsening, and Black Bermudians spoke out against the injustices.

In 1946, the Bermuda Workers Association presented a petition to the British government asking for an investigation into the treatment of Black and working-class white Bermudians. This new spotlight on human rights continued with a Parliamentary Interracial Committee appointed in 1953.

Young Black activists organized the secret Progressive Group. They confronted segregation head-on and called for an island-wide boycott of theaters in 1959. The goal of the Theatre Boycott was to bring an end to separate seating areas in movie theaters, many of which reserved the better balcony seats for white patrons and required Black patrons to sit below. Over a period of two weeks, the nonviolent boycott grew. People gathered nightly to speak out against segregation. The pressure of this activism forced the theaters to close. By the time theaters agreed to desegregate seating, many of Bermuda's churches, hotels, and restaurants had already announced their intention to desegregate as well. Segregation in restaurants became illegal in 1961.

The fight for equality continued into the 1960s. Black Bermudians pushed for desegregated schools, universal voting rights, equal economic opportunities, and fair labor laws. By 1961, property restrictions for voting were removed. However, progress through legislation was slow. The Bermuda Electric Light Company (BELCO) workers' strike in 1965 took a bloody turn, and tensions kept mounting until the 1968 Floral Day Pageant riot. Violent encounters between the police and young Black Bermudians threw the island into a state of emergency. British troops, who had left Bermuda in 1957, temporarily returned to the island to enforce order.

In 1968, a new constitution was passed for Bermuda. It stated that Bermuda was protected under the umbrella of the British Commonwealth but would govern itself. The constitution also outlined civil rights for all Bermudians.

Racial tensions continued to underlie the major political changes of the 1970s. Bermudian schools were desegregated in 1971, but labor strikes and riots continued to draw attention to the economic disadvantages of Black Bermudians. Amid this tense climate, in 1972, Sir Richard Sharples, a white man, became governor of Bermuda. On March 10, 1973, Sharples and his aide Hugh Sayers were assassinated outside Bermuda's Government House.

Erskine Durrant "Buck" Burrows and Larry Tacklyn, two Black men, were convicted of Sharples's murder and other similar murders. Burrows confessed to killing Sharples as a form of anticolonial protest, stating, "The motive for killing the Governor was to seek to make the people, black people in particular, become aware of the evilness and wickedness of the colonialist system in this island." Bermudians were shocked by Sharples's murder, but many worked to spare Burrows and Tacklyn from the death penalty. More than 13,000 people signed a petition for their reprieve. When the execution went forward anyway in 1977, it sparked 48 hours of island-wide protest, arson, and violence.

The push for equality kept building through the following decades. The 1981 Human Rights Act legally banned discrimination based on race, gender, age, and other differences. Racial tensions have always been present in Bermuda, but progress continues toward equity. Today, social justice activists

The British navy maintained a presence at the Royal Naval Dockyard from 1809 to 1976. Now, the Dockyard is a civic center.

in Bermuda focus on racial disparities in employment, educational access, and criminal justice.

TIES TO THE UNITED KINGDOM

For years, Bermudians have debated how to continue their relationship with the United Kingdom. Although they have been self-governing since 1957 when Britain withdrew its military forces, Bermuda is still part of the United Kingdom. The official leader is still the British monarch, and daily life and government are mainly modeled after English ways.

In 1995, three-fourths of Bermudians voted to maintain their relationship with the United Kingdom. Bermuda's ties to the United Kingdom were reasserted in 2002 when the British Overseas Territories Act granted full British citizenship to citizens of Bermuda. A commission addressed the question and potential procedures of achieving independence from the United Kingdom in 2004, but public support for independence was again lacking.

In 2009, Bermuda celebrated its 400th anniversary with local festivities and a three-day royal visit from Queen Elizabeth II and her husband, the Duke of Edinburgh. Although the question of Bermuda's political status as a British territory is likely to be repeatedly revisited, cultural ties to Britain remain an important element of life in Bermuda.

UNEXPECTED CRISIS

Bermuda has weathered storms, global wars, and internal conflicts for over 400 years as a British territory. Like many countries, the greatest challenge to Bermuda in the 21st century has been the COVID-19 pandemic, which first affected the island in March 2020. Bermuda mobilized its public health response with closures, lockdowns, curfews, travel restrictions, quarantine guidelines, and vaccinations. As a country dependent on tourism, the pandemic, which halted international travel, strained Bermuda's service-based economy. The lightening of restrictions in the spring of 2021 was seen as a positive sign for the country.

INTERNET LINKS

bnt.bm
The website of the Bermuda National Trust includes links to and information about important cultural heritage sites in Bermuda.

nmb.bm
Visit the website of the National Museum of Bermuda to read about archaeological discoveries and artifacts that shed light on Bermuda's history.

GOVERNMENT

The small British Union Jack on its flag points to
Bermuda's status as the oldest British Overseas Territory.

JUST LOOKING AT BERMUDA'S national flag can tell you a lot about the history of the country and its connection to the United Kingdom. The flag has had a bright red background since 1967. In the upper left corner is a British Union Jack that represents Bermuda's ties to the Crown. On the right is Bermuda's coat of arms. It is a white and green shield with a red lion holding an illustration of the *Sea Venture*, the ship that brought English colonists to Bermuda.

Bermuda's close relationship with the United Kingdom has been redefined several times. Bermuda became an English (later British) colony in its first days as a settled island. Its Parliament was given certain lawmaking powers beginning in 1620, but Bermuda was still under colonial control. After the introduction of its first constitution in 1968, Bermuda became a self-governing entity. Bermuda is now a British Overseas Territory, which was formerly known as a Crown Colony or a British Dependent Territory. Full independence from the United Kingdom has never been sought, despite heated discussions and differing political opinions. Whenever the topic has been put to a vote, the majority has opted to keep their ties to the Crown.

BRITISH OVERSEAS TERRITORY

As a British Overseas Territory, Bermuda relies on the United Kingdom for defense, security, and foreign affairs. Bermuda is represented by the United Kingdom in the United Nations and international embassies. The British monarch is the Chief of State of Bermuda and appoints the local governor. In addition, any changes to Bermuda's constitution must be approved by Britain.

Bermuda is a parliamentary democracy like the United Kingdom, but it has its own constitution and laws. As a result, Bermuda's social and political world has evolved separately from Britain: Women first voted in 1944; the first election based on universal suffrage was held in 1968; racial segregation ended in schools in 1971; Burrows and Tacklyn were put to death in Bermuda in 1977, even though Britain abolished capital punishment in 1965; the Supreme Court legalized same-sex marriage in 2018. When comparing these milestones with the United Kingdom, Bermuda has often been slow to change.

GOVERNMENT BRANCHES

Bermuda's constitution, adopted in 1968, outlines three branches of government in the parliamentary democracy: executive, legislative, and judicial. The executive branch includes the head of state, the premier and Cabinet, and the governor. In Bermuda's case, the head of state is the British monarch, currently Queen Elizabeth II. She is in charge of appointing the governor. The governor, in turn, is responsible for external affairs, internal security, the police, and defense.

The premier is the head of the government and leader of the majority party. The premier nominates up to 12 legislators from the House of Assembly and one or two from the Senate to serve on the Cabinet. There must be at least seven Cabinet members, including the premier. Cabinet members are given the title "minister" and are responsible for different government departments. Cabinet meetings are private, and all decisions are made unanimously by the ministers. Most executive power in the government rests with the Cabinet, as the governor and monarch's roles are more ceremonial than administrative.

Bermudian citizenship is difficult to attain. Even children born in Bermuda are not officially Bermudian unless one parent is native to the country. No outsider can become a Bermudian, gain citizenship, vote, or buy real estate unless they marry a Bermudian and live with that person for more than 10 years. This is the only democratic country in the world with these rules.

Since 2002, Bermudian citizens have been automatically granted full British citizenship by the British Overseas Territories Act. This means that native Bermudians can more easily study, work, and live in Britain. Naturalized Bermudians (those who have gained citizenship through marriage) are eligible, but they have to apply for British citizenship.

The legislative branch consists of the Senate and the House of Assembly. The Senate is made up of 11 members; each member serves a 3-year term. The Senate is often referred to as the Upper House. All senators are appointed by the governor: Five are recommended by the premier, three are recommended by the opposition party, and three are chosen directly by the governor. The House of Assembly, or Lower House, has 36 members who are elected through popular vote. They serve for up to five years. Many House of Assembly members also hold full-time jobs outside of government. All meetings of the House and Senate are open to the public, and debates have been broadcasted on the radio since 1991. For a bill to pass into law, it must be approved by both the Assembly and the Senate before being sent to the governor, who signs it. When a law is passed, it becomes an Act of Parliament.

The judicial branch consists of the Supreme Court, Court of Appeal, and Magistrates Court. Members are appointed by the Bermudian government rather than elected by the people. The chief justice is the head of this branch. Judges in all Bermudian courtrooms wear formal robes and long, white powdered wigs in keeping with the English tradition.

Bermuda's House of Assembly and Supreme Court meet in the stately Sessions House in Hamilton. In 1887, a clock tower was designed to honor the Golden Jubilee of Queen Victoria.

ONE PERSON, ONE VOTE

Just before emancipation, Bermudian lawmakers introduced new property requirements for voting or running for Parliament that were designed to limit the civic participation of Black Bermudians. Citizens who did not own valuable property were barred from voting from 1834 until 1961. In addition, wealthy citizens with property in more than one parish were permitted to cast multiple votes.

Suffrage movements campaigned to fix these imbalances. One of the first suffrage movements focused on votes for women. Women, regardless of property ownership, were prohibited from voting. An early wave of activity for women's suffrage failed in 1890, but the movement was revived in the years after World War I. Gladys Misick Morrell was a leading figure in this struggle; she was inspired by the work of British suffragettes. Morrell founded the Bermuda Woman Suffrage Society and organized the campaign for over 20 years. A yearly protest took place when female property owners refused to pay taxes. In response, their furniture was seized by local authorities and auctioned off to pay the taxes. These public showdowns brought attention to the Suffrage Society.

After women served bravely in World War II, Parliament began to warm to their cause. A 1944 bill granted the right to vote to women who owned property. Four years later, Bermuda elected its first two female lawmakers to the House of Assembly.

Pressure to change the property requirements for all men and women mounted in the next decades. As Bermuda's public spaces began to desegregate in 1959, many people called out oppressive voting restrictions. In 1960, the Committee for Universal Adult Suffrage (CUAS) came together and committed to months of campaigning.

The tide turned in June 1961 when Parliament passed the Franchise Bill. This granted voting rights to all Bermudian adults. However, some wealthy property owners were still entitled to a "plus vote." When the Bermuda Constitution was adopted in 1968, it finally struck out the "plus vote" and granted one vote to every citizen. Today, all Bermudian citizens age 18 and older are eligible to vote.

Black men in Bermuda who owned property were able to vote and occupy elected offices at a time when all women, Black or white, were barred from voting. Some Black politicians, like Dr. Eustace McCann in the House of Assembly, worried that opening the vote to property-owning women would only cement the harmful property requirements. However, McCann voted to pass the women's suffrage bill in 1944.

He said, "When one speaks about keeping the vote from women on the basis of sex, one must also think about keeping certain people from getting jobs because of the colour of their skin … I shall vote for this measure today because I hate to see any group enslaved by the power of others and refused their legitimate rights. I call on all Assemblymen to consider these matters that would grant to others the same privileges now proposed for the Suffrage Society."

POLITICAL PARTIES

The 1968 constitution laid out the system of a majority government for Bermuda. This means that the political party that has won the most seats in the House of Assembly—the majority party—forms the government and their leader becomes premier. The second largest political party represented in the House of Assembly becomes the opposition party.

In 1963, the Progressive Labour Party became the first political party in Bermuda. It mainly represented the Black labor movement. The following year, the more conservative United Bermuda Party was founded. It was often criticized for reinforcing the power of a small, elite, mostly white group.

The United Bermuda Party won elections and formed the government from 1964 until 1998. A major change came when the Progressive Labour Party became the majority party from 1998 to 2012.

The United Bermuda Party and another group called the Bermuda Democratic Alliance joined together within the One Bermuda Alliance in 2012. The One Bermuda Alliance won the elections that year and formed the government for five years. However, the 2017 election placed the Progressive Labour Party back at the helm under the leadership of Premier David Burt.

GOVERNMENT BUILDINGS

The city of Hamilton is the seat of Bermuda's government.

The capital of Bermuda was moved to the city of Hamilton in 1815. Now, Hamilton is the site of most government-related buildings. The Sessions House in Hamilton is an Italian-style building constructed in 1819. The House of Assembly and the Supreme Court meet there. The House of Assembly's chambers are similar to the British House of Commons. The two major political parties sit across from each other and are presided over by the Speaker in a long black robe and powdered wig, with a cedar gavel in hand. A gold-plated mace is carried into the chamber when the Speaker enters and exits as a sign of their authority.

The Cabinet Building is also in Hamilton and houses the Senate. The building was designed in 1837 and opened in 1884. Tourists like to stand in front of the building on the first Friday of November. This is the day for the formal opening of Parliament, a ritual that dates back many years. It is one of the few occasions when the House of Assembly and Senate meet jointly.

The governor arrives in a fancy carriage drawn by huge black horses and led by a police escort. Wearing a plumed hat and the regalia of their position, they enter the building. A senior officer carries a black rod made by the Crown jewelers; the officer asks the Speaker of the House and Senate members to begin. The governor then gives what's known as the Throne Speech from a very small throne made out of cedar that dates back to 1642.

BERMUDA'S OMBUDSMAN

Her Excellency Ms. Rena Lalgie was sworn in as governor of Bermuda in 2020.

The word "ombudsman" itself is derived from a Swedish word meaning "representative," and an ombudsman has an important role in representing Bermuda's best interests. An ombudsman is an independent official with the responsibility of listening and responding to complaints from the public about the authorities, including the government and boards or bodies appointed and/or funded by the legislature. If people feel they were somehow treated unfairly or dishonestly, they take their complaint to the ombudsman. This person has to be neutral at all times and thus is sometimes referred to as a "critical friend to both" sides. More than 100 countries today employ at least one ombudsman.

In Bermuda, the ombudsman is appointed by the governor after discussion with the premier. Bermuda's first ombudsman, Arlene Brock, was appointed in 2004. "I think that the public took us onboard quite seriously," Brock said after two years in the position. The type of complaints Brock handled ranged from a person missing money from the Department of Social Services to the Bermuda Housing Corporation receiving double payments from some of its properties. Brock served until 2014, when Victoria R. M. Pearman became Bermuda's second ombudsman.

MILITARY

As an overseas territory, Bermuda falls under the protection of the British Armed Forces. Locally, they also rely on the Bermuda Police Service and the Royal Bermuda Regiment to keep Bermudians safe and secure.

The Royal Bermuda Regiment has a long history that can be traced to local militias in Bermuda's earliest days as a colony. In 1895, the formal organization of military units took place in order to support the British army garrison. As the island was deeply segregated at the time, two separate units were established. The Bermuda Militia Artillery (BMA) was made up of Black soldiers, and the Bermuda Volunteer Rifle Corps (BVRC) consisted of white volunteers. Both units served in World War I and World War II. In 1965, the two segregated units were joined to create the Royal Bermuda Regiment. Throughout the following decades, the regiment responded to riots, labor strikes, and national disasters to preserve order and safety.

As of 2021, the Royal Bermuda Regiment was made up of about 350 men and women. Their main role is to help the police maintain internal security and engage in disaster management. In recent years, the regiment has been mobilized to provide natural disaster relief and humanitarian aid after hurricanes. The regiment has also assisted some of Bermuda's Atlantic neighbors, including the Cayman Islands, Grenada, and Turks and Caicos. In 2017, the regiment provided two months of service to prepare for and secure the 35th America's Cup yacht racing event that took place in Bermuda.

In the past, serving with the Royal Bermuda Regiment was mandatory for a random selection of young men between the ages of 18 and 25. However, all members of the regiment since 2016 have been volunteers. Male and female citizens in good health, between the ages of 18 and 45, and without a criminal record are eligible to volunteer. Training is provided for those in the regiment, and members serve on a part-time basis for an initial period of three years and two months.

One of the best times to see the Royal Bermuda Regiment is during the Beating Retreat ceremony, which is performed at least once a month and even more often during the summer. Led by the Royal Bermuda Regiment Band and Corps of Drums, the members dress in full uniform: red coats, blue pants, and white pith helmets. Often, they are accompanied by the Bermuda Islands Pipe Band and Dancers.

The Royal Bermuda Regiment can also be spotted at the Queen's Birthday Parade in June as they march along Front Street to the sound of cannons firing a salute and the band playing music and keeping time. As the regiment passes by the governor, they salute. They repeat this march in November for Remembrance Day.

In 2020, Bermuda's military expanded through the creation of the first Bermuda Coast Guard Unit. The new unit is undertaking maritime security formerly performed by the Bermuda Police Service. They operate around the clock to provide safety and rescue operations as needed near the shores of Bermuda.

INTERNET LINKS

ukota.org
Bermuda is a member of the United Kingdom Overseas Territories Association (UKOTA), represented on this website, which was established in 1994 to unify the interests of the territories.

www.bermudaregiment.bm/about/history
Watch a short video about the history of the Royal Bermuda Regiment on its official website.

www.gov.bm
Bermuda's official government website offers descriptions of how the government functions, plus current news and information.

www.parliament.bm
The Bermuda Parliament website includes bios of current lawmakers, news, and information about how Parliament works.

www.royal.uk
Visit the website of the United Kingdom's monarchy, with information about the queen and the Commonwealth.

ECONOMY

Bermuda left behind the British currency of pounds, shillings, and pence in 1970. In its place, it adopted the Bermuda dollar.

4

FROM ITS EARLIEST YEARS, Bermuda's economy was based on the business of shipbuilding. Bermudians were known throughout many areas of the world for their ability to build sloops and schooners that moved faster across the water than those made by other shipbuilders. These speedy ships could arrive far ahead of competitors and transport cargo, legally and illegally. Bermuda sloops sailed far and wide, gaining a reputation for greatness on both sides of the Atlantic Ocean. The British and French used Bermuda sloops as carrier and mail boats, and American colonists used them throughout the American Revolution, when Bermuda was producing about 100 sloops a year. However, when a disease ruined most of the island's cedar trees and steel ships became more popular, the demand for these ships plummeted.

Bermudian and U.S. currency are of equal value and can both be used in Bermuda.

Shipping goods from Bermuda's docks has been a consistent feature of the island's economy.

A bouquet of Bermuda lilies is traditionally sent to Queen Elizabeth every Easter.

Maritime activities like salt trading and whaling were important industries that also peaked in the 1700s. Like shipbuilding, salt raking in the Turks Islands relied heavily on the work of enslaved laborers. Mary Prince, who later published the account of her life of enslavement, suffered cruelly as an enslaved salt raker.

In the 1800s, agriculture became dominant. Bermudian onions were exported in vast quantities. Easter lilies also became a profitable crop for sale, and exports started in the 1880s. By the end of the century, Bermuda's bulbs made up about 90 percent of the Easter lily market in the United States. The elegant lilies were well-suited to Bermuda's climate, at least until a virus nearly wiped out Bermuda's 204 lily fields in the 1920s. The lilies recovered, but they are now primarily grown to add beauty to Bermuda's gardens.

Agricultural failures and the declining demand for Bermuda's exported goods in the United States led to a new focus on tourism. Fortunately, Bermuda's

Cedar sloops made the activities of early Bermudian fishermen, salt traders, privateers, and smugglers possible. This fast ship was typically constructed with a long and narrow body, one mast, and triangular sails. Native Bermudian red cedar gave strength, durability, and speed to sloops. Most were crafted and constructed by free and enslaved Black Bermudians.

Sloops carried Bermudians to the salt beds of the Turks Islands and then delivered that salt to ports in Newfoundland and New England. Their speed helped the Royal Navy chase down slave ships in the Caribbean in its quest to break up the Atlantic slave trade. Smugglers, pirates, and privateers also relied on the quickness of their sloops to help them acquire goods at sea.

In the 1820s, shipbuilders in New England and Maryland adapted the Bermudian sloop model to make their own vessels. Bermuda's shipbuilding business declined soon after. A dwindling population of cedar trees was the final blow to Bermuda's once-thriving sloop business.

beautiful scenery and comfortable climate drew tourists to its shores. Tourism was the mainstay of the islands for the rest of the 20th century. In the 21st century, it has been largely replaced in importance by Bermuda's attraction as an offshore financial center.

ONION MANIA

In the 1850s, shipbuilding gave way to a new economic activity: growing and exporting onions. The humble onion had been grown in Bermuda since the days of the *Sea Venture*, but it was not until the 1800s that agricultural practices improved enough on the islands to create a Bermuda onion boom. At that time, skilled Portuguese immigrant farmers introduced new farming techniques that nurtured the growth of tasty Bermuda onions.

The first, historic shipment of Bermuda onions was exported from St. George's port to the United States in 1847. By the end of the century, shiploads of Bermuda onions were flooding the markets of the United States and England. Sadly, World War I made shipping in the Atlantic dangerous. By

A LANDMARK HOTEL

One hotel and tourist destination that has been involved in Bermuda's history for more than a century is the Hamilton Princess Hotel. Construction began in 1884, and the hotel opened its doors in January 1885. Now called the Hamilton Princess and Beach Club, the hotel offers luxury accommodations and access to Bermuda's famous pink sand beaches.

Throughout its history, the hotel has hosted celebrities, politicians, and authors. Mark Twain was a familiar sight to early guests of the hotel. He was known to read aloud from his works and sign autographs during his visits.

When World War II diminished tourism significantly, the hotel closed to visitors. For five years, it served as headquarters for the British intelligence operation in the Atlantic. The operation was supervised by Sir William Stephenson, better known by his code name Intrepid. As many as 1,200 people worked in this hotel during the war, searching for spy messages in the mail.

the time trade could safely resume, American farmers in Texas were growing their own onions and shipping them to other states by rail. Bermuda onion exports steadily fell before coming to a halt in 1946.

Bermuda onions are still dearly valued on their home islands. In the 1850s, Bermuda gained the nickname "the Onion Patch," and its residents are still proudly called "Onions." Bermuda Onion Day is celebrated with creative recipes and competitions every May in St. David's.

VISITING PARADISE

In the second half of the 19th century, people began traveling to Bermuda for leisure and to see what island life was like. They wanted to walk the beaches, enjoy the weather, and explore the parishes. Construction of hotels began, and roads and towns expanded to make room for these new visitors.

One of the best-known visitors was Princess Louise, the daughter of Queen Victoria. In 1883, she came to Bermuda and stayed for several months. Normally, she lived in Canada with her husband, the governor-general, and she was eager to put the Canadian cold behind her. Princess Louise was the

first royal person to set foot on the island. She described Bermuda as a place of "eternal Spring." The Princess Hotel in Hamilton opened two years later and was named in her honor. Princess Louise's visit started a new trend of tourism to the island.

Visitors flocked to Bermuda at the turn of the 20th century on steamships from New York and Canada. They came in search of gorgeous scenery, an escape from busy city life, or a climate that promoted good health. However, just as tourism took off, World War I began, and travel stopped altogether. Fortunately, England's Furness Steamship Company chose Bermuda as one of its cruise-liner stops after the war. Its frequent stops helped Bermuda's economy to rally, and the island sailed through the 1920s and 1930s, while other countries struggled through the years of the Great Depression.

Tourism was Bermuda's main economic resource for most of the 20th century. Like many other places across the world, it saw a dramatic dip in the number of travelers following the terrorist attacks of September 11, 2001, and during the global recession in 2008 and 2009. Slowly,

The town of St. George, which was founded in 1612, was named a UNESCO World Heritage site in 2000.

Take a look at a Bermuda penny today and you will see the image of a hog engraved on it. When English settlers came to Bermuda, hogs—first deposited on the island to multiply as a food source for shipwrecked or seafaring explorers—were some of the most numerous animals they saw. King James I granted Bermuda permission to mint the first colonial coins in 1615. They were made from copper and had an image of a hog on one side and a ship on the other. The coins became unpopular since they could not be used off of the island, and they were rarely found after 1650. In 1970, Bermuda adopted its own new currency. The penny bears an image of a hog on one side as a nod to Bermuda's history.

however, the number of visitors began to climb again. Statistics from the Bermuda Tourism Authority show that in 2019, a record-setting number of tourists—about 808,000 people—came to the island to visit, do business, or get married. This is a particularly amazing number when you consider that it is more than 10 times the population of Bermuda itself.

The majority of tourists come from the United States, and the rest tend to be from Canada and Great Britain. In 2018, tourists spent more than $500 million on hotel accommodations, dining at restaurants, visiting tourist attractions, and purchasing products in Bermuda. Bermuda has been a favorite honeymoon stop for decades, and it is full of wedding venues and planners who can show couples how to fill out the necessary paperwork and get married in local churches, in hotels, at historic sites, at parks, or right on the beach. In 2018, more than 60 percent of the weddings that took place in Bermuda were for nonresidents.

A FINANCIAL CENTER

As successful as tourism has been for Bermuda, recent years have found an even better source of revenue for the country: foreign businesses. In 1997, China took over Hong Kong from Britain. As a result, Bermuda suddenly became the most populous British territory at that time. Bermudian government officials convinced many of the foreign companies who had headquarters in Hong Kong to come to Bermuda. By 2000, about half of the companies that had been on the Hong Kong stock exchange were relocated to Bermuda. For the first time in a century, tourism dropped to the second source of revenue.

Since 2000, the number of international companies with branches in Bermuda has expanded. According to various financial reports, around 75 percent of the U.S. Fortune 500 companies are registered in Bermuda. More than 16,000 businesses are registered there, although only a small number actually operate in Bermuda. They are primarily insurance and reinsurance companies and investment firms. Many companies register in Bermuda because there are no corporation or income taxes on the island. If companies register in Bermuda but are based in their home countries, the tax benefits can amount to hundreds of thousands—even millions—of dollars in savings. At the same time, Bermuda benefits through job creation and government fees.

This arrangement can be a source of tension with other countries, although Bermuda has tax information exchange agreements with many foreign governments. Despite the existence of a tax treaty with Bermuda, President Joe Biden of the United States found fault with this international relationship. In a 2021 speech to the U.S. Congress, Biden named Bermuda as a tax haven and proposed the institution of a global minimum tax.

TRADE

A third source of business in Bermuda is the process of exporting and importing. Since land is so limited, Bermudians must import a great deal of what they need. Food, clothing, furniture, fuel, appliances, and cars are imported on a regular basis. In 2019, about 44 percent of imports came from the United States, 17 percent from South Korea, 10 percent from Germany, and 8 percent from Canada.

At the same time, the island is busy exporting cargo, such as pharmaceuticals, paint, alcohol (especially rum) and other beverages, and perfume. In 2017, 49 percent of exports went to Jamaica, 36 percent to Luxumbourg, and about 5 percent to the United States. Exports led to $19 million of the gross domestic product (GDP) that year.

In 2020, Premier David Burt said the United States was "Bermuda's largest and most important trading partner." Other major trading partners are the European Union, Canada, and the islands of the Caribbean.

EMPLOYMENT

Bermuda is a place with high average incomes and low levels of poverty. Despite its small size, Bermuda has a very stable economy. Bermuda's GDP in 2019 was $7.48 billion. International business makes up 85 percent of Bermuda's GDP, and tourism accounts for 5 percent. Agriculture, construction, and fishing are also small-scale industries.

The labor force in 2016 was made up of 33,480 citizens. Most, about 85 percent, worked in the service sector. Another 13 percent were employed in industry, and 2 percent worked in agriculture. The unemployment rate in 2017 was 7 percent.

Unemployment in Bermuda is generally low, and there is a legal reason why. There is a law in Bermuda stating that as long as there is a Bermudian available to do a job or fill a position, a business owner cannot hire a non-Bermudian.

Poverty is rare as well. In 2016, the average annual income for a household in Bermuda was $131,074, far higher than many other countries. It is also necessary, as the cost of living is very high. Housing prices are often three times what they are in the United States or Canada, and interest rates are usually several points higher. Such a small island nation does not have room for any new housing, so any homes on the market usually sell at steep prices and often go to wealthy non-Bermudians. In addition, although Bermuda does not have income or sales tax, it does have real-estate taxes. Owning a home is costly, and many Bermudians rent property instead. About 52 percent of households in Bermuda rent their homes. For those who struggle financially, the government offers programs like housing allowances and rent control to make affording a home possible.

PANDEMIC EFFECTS

The COVID-19 pandemic posed unexpected challenges for all Bermudians in 2020 and 2021. Travel restrictions put a halt to tourism, businesses closed, and many workers were temporarily unemployed. According to the Bermuda Tourist Authority, the number of visitors fell from 808,000 in 2019 to 53,000 in 2020.

Bermuda spent $125 million on its COVID-19 response in 2020, and the government paid more than $60 million in unemployment benefits to Bermudians. In January 2021, the government received its first COVID-19 vaccine doses and put a strategy into action to vaccinate at least 60 percent of the population. Businesses began opening up again in the spring of 2021.

In the midst of the pandemic, the government introduced the Work from Bermuda Certificate. This offers the opportunity for university students or professionals studying or working remotely to live in Bermuda for up to one year. The certificate is meant to boost the economy by drawing long-term visitors to the island.

INTERNET LINKS

data.worldbank.org/country/BM
View the most recent economic statistics from Bermuda on the World Bank's website.

whc.unesco.org/en/list/983/
Learn why the historic town of St. George and its fortifications were selected as a UNESCO World Heritage site.

www.bma.bm
The Bermuda Monetary Authority regulates finances in Bermuda by overseeing banks and the Bermuda Stock Exchange.

www.gotobermuda.com
Bermuda's official travel website highlights some of the most popular spots for tourism.

ENVIRONMENT

A variety of coral species are protected by Bermuda's Department of Environment and Natural Resources.

5

ENVIRONMENTAL STEWARDSHIP IN Bermuda requires careful decision-making and planning. In many ways, the islands are not naturally equipped to support modern human life. There are no natural fresh water sources on the island, and disposing of waste safely is challenging.

In addition, intense human activity and high populations have damaged the islands. Bermuda's forests have largely been cleared to make way for agriculture and housing and to supply Bermuda's industries. This imbalance in the natural ecosystem creates its own problems of erosion, water run-off, and vulnerability to storms. Invasive species have wiped out many native plants and animals. Global climate change threatens the islands with rising sea levels and the risk of increasingly intense tropical storms.

Fortunately, the Bermudian government and its citizens are committed to preserving Bermuda's natural beauty for future generations. Ample funds and resources have been dedicated to safeguarding Bermuda's natural environment. Many parks and 12 nature reserves are dispersed across Bermuda to protect beaches, green spaces, and natural habitats.

Bermuda passed the New World's first environmental conservation laws in the early 1600s.

If people are going to spend a vacation in Bermuda, they should bring their walking shoes. Only Bermudians are permitted to drive traditional cars in Bermuda, and they must follow a strict set of rules for car use. There are many other alternatives, of course. People can take a ride on city buses, jump on a ferry, or grab a local taxi. Many tourists choose to walk or bicycle (Bermudians call these pedal bikes) from place to place. Travelers can also rent a scooter or a tiny, two-seat, electric car called a Renault Twizy to get around the islands. Just remember, Bermudians drive on the left side of the road!

CURBING POLLUTION

Visitors to Bermuda often notice that it seems very clean, from the city streets to the parks. This is primarily because Bermuda has rather stiff anti-litter laws. It also has an annual garbage cleanup campaign that many people and organizations participate in, collecting tons of trash in a short period of time. You will not find graffiti dashed across the walls or anywhere else, either, as it is also banned.

In addition to these rules, there are important restrictions on cars. With so little room, it would take only a few cars to pollute Bermuda's air and clog its streets. To help prevent air pollution, families are only allowed to own one automobile. However, households can have additional motorcycles or scooters for getting around. Many businesses are also only allowed one truck for making deliveries. Even with these rules in place, Bermuda has one of the highest rates in the world of automobiles per square mile, and traffic jams are a common sight. The government has encouraged a greater reliance on electric cars and energy-efficient motorcycles, ride-sharing, and public transportation to curb the use of fossil fuels.

REUSING AND RECYCLING

In April 2007, a new program began in Bermuda known as TAG, or Tin, Aluminum and Glass. The government hoped that TAG would remind people to recycle their waste. The launch of the TAG program coincided with the opening of a recycling center that crushes tin and aluminum into bales sold to the United States to produce sheet metal. Glass is reused in Bermuda to create a drainage material on golf courses, landscaped areas, and large construction sites.

Household waste is collected every week and converted into electricity. Household waste includes paper, cardboard, plastics, and food waste. Once the waste is delivered to the Tynes Bay Waste-to-Energy Facility, it is burned to create electricity. The government also encourages residents to process food waste in home and backyard composters to create nutrient-rich soil.

WASTE AND WATER

Bermudians have historically struggled to safely dispose of trash on their small archipelago. Although the government has systems in place to process trash and recycle electronics and appliances, items are sometimes illegally dumped in towns, marshes, caves, and fields. It is not unusual for toxins to leak from these sites or for pieces of plastic to make their way into the ocean, where they threaten turtles, seabirds, and even whales. Fines for dumping can be as high as $10,000, but the problem continues.

Sewage is another source of concern for the environment. Bermuda does not have any central sewage system. Homes need to have cesspits dug to contain household waste, including detergents, pharmaceuticals, and microorganisms. They have to be far away from the home's water tanks to be safe. They have to be cleaned out on a regular basis, and they can cause terrible problems if they leak or are damaged. Sewage from homes and businesses in the larger cities of Hamilton and St. George, plus the sewage from many cruise ships, is often pumped directly into the ocean. This contaminates the water and threatens the health of coral reefs and marine life.

In 2020, the Ministry of Public Works presented the outline of a new Waste and Water Recovery Utility. A sewage treatment plant would collect waste that is currently pumped into the marine environment. The sewage would be processed into non-potable water that could be used for flushing toilets, irrigation, and other uses that do not require potable water. The remaining sludge could be incinerated in the Waste-to-Energy Facility to create more electricity. In turn, that electricity could be used to power the Sea Water Reverse Osmosis plant that turns sea water into potable water. This plan would not only treat waste and sewage as a renewable resource to power the island and provide drinking water, but it would also reduce pollution in the ocean.

MANAGING HURRICANES

Hurricanes are an environmental emergency that Bermuda occasionally encounters. Compared to other islands, Bermuda usually escapes major damage from the storms. One of the worst hurricanes hit in 1926 with winds of 125 miles (201 km) per hour. In 1987, Hurricane Emily hit Bermuda, injuring 70 people and costing millions of dollars in damage. Hurricane Fabian struck in 2003, the most powerful storm to hit in 50 years. Four people drowned, trees were knocked down, and the island endured $300 million in damages. Since then, Hurricanes Bertha in 2008, Fay and Gonzalo in 2014, Joaquin in 2015, and Nicole in 2016 have also caused damage in Bermuda. Hurricane Paulette directly hit the island in 2020, knocking out power with heavy wind and rain.

The frequent storms that blow through the Atlantic are hard on the island in other ways also. High winds cause waves that push against the rocky shore. As pieces of rock fall off, the nests and habitats of coastal creatures like the longtail and cahow are often destroyed.

PROTECTING NATURE

Bermuda passed its first environmental conservation legislation in 1616 with a law protecting local birds, including the cahow. A 1620 law aimed to protect young green sea turtles from hunting, and a 1622 law placed limits on cedar harvesting. By the time these laws took effect, it was nearly too late to save the native species.

In 1949 and 1975, the Bermuda government passed other laws to protect the island's birds. It was not until March of 2004, however, that it passed the Protected Species Act, which calls for a proactive approach to saving threatened species and habitats. The current list of protected species covers birds like the longtail and cahow, all marine mammals including whales and dolphins, reptiles like the Bermuda skink and green turtle, the Bermuda land snail, the leaf-cutter bee, a wide variety of coral species, and a host of plants.

An incredible number of invasive plant species have taken over in different parts of Bermuda, pushing out the native plants. Invasive species pose some of the greatest threats to Bermuda's biodiversity. Invasive plants, which were not natural in the habitat, can change light levels, decrease oxygen in water, change soil chemistry, and increase surface runoff and erosion. They can also kill off endemic and native species until they are extinct. Examples of these harmful plant species include Brazil pepper, allspice, fiddlewood, Chinese fan palm, and Surinam cherry.

Many environmental problems are the accidental result of attempts to fix other problems. Like a row of dominoes, one problem leads directly to another. For example, Bermuda has the only native population of Eastern bluebirds outside of mainland North America. However, the number of bluebirds has diminished, in part because of pesticides and competition with sparrows and kiskadees. Sparrows and kiskadees are not native species; they were brought to the area to help get rid of the anole lizards. The lizards were brought to the

Some early Bermudians depended on whaling for their livelihood. Today, humpback whales and all marine mammals are protected species.

Eastern bluebirds can no longer survive in Bermuda without the help of special nest boxes that protect them from invasive predators and competitors.

THE BERMUDA CEDAR

The first humans to land on Bermuda came to a place of lush forests bursting with trees like the Bermuda cedar. As people settled on the islands, they introduced activities, pests, invasive plants, and diseases that diminished the forests. Early explorers released pigs to multiply into an abundant food source, but the pigs uprooted the forest floor in their quest for food. Rats from ships also disturbed the forest's natural cycle by eating seeds. Settlers cleared the forests to make room for agriculture or to supply timber for shipbuilding and construction.

The Bermuda cedar suffered from all of these factors, but the introduction of a pest in the 1940s nearly wiped it out. Two kinds of virus-spreading insects, called oystershell scale and cedar scale, arrived in Bermuda. Between 1946 and 1951, 95 percent of Bermuda cedars died. It is estimated that cedar scale killed around 3 million trees.

island to control the Mediterranean fruit fly. The kiskadees are also responsible for the extinction of the Bermuda cicada. In addition, the anole lizards ate beneficial insects that could have stopped the spread of a kind of insect called a scale that nearly destroyed Bermuda cedars. In this way, introducing new species can disrupt an ecosystem and cause a chain of harmful imbalances that threaten native and endemic species.

Other environmental problems include overfishing around the islands. Overfishing occurs when too many fish are caught, upsetting the delicate balance in the sea of predators and prey. As a result, the government has put fishing limits in place for certain species.

The delicate coral reefs are also being threatened. Tourists eager to take pieces home with them and boats that come too close or run aground can damage the reefs. A number of these boats are also covered in toxic paints that contain copper, a biocide, or product designed to kill microorganisms, including coral. Boat mooring chains, anchors, and propellers also damage sea-grass beds and reefs.

So far, Bermuda coral has proven somewhat resilient to the rising sea temperatures that result from global climate change. Coral species around Florida and the Caribbean have been hugely damaged by bleaching, a response to higher water temperatures in which corals shed the helpful algae that grow on them. Fortunately, the coral reefs around Bermuda have been only minimally affected by bleaching.

Bermuda has the largest population of longtails– about 2,000 to 3,000 birds–in the Atlantic.

SIGNATURE SPECIES

A pest wiped out most of the cedar trees that are perfectly suited to Bermuda's island habitat and climate. Fortunately, a small portion of the Bermuda cedars were resistant to the disaster. They have been bred in an effort to rehabilitate this important species. In recent years, there has been a strong effort to replant cedars, though progress is slow.

The national symbol for Bermuda used to be the white-tailed tropic bird, more commonly known as the longtail. It is a yellow-billed, white-tailed bird with striking black markings across its back and wings. The longtail's image can be found on all kinds of souvenirs and currency throughout the island.

The longtail lives at sea in the winter and returns to Bermuda to nest from May through September.

A WELCOME RETURN

At one time, Bermuda's beaches offered safe havens for a variety of turtles to lay their eggs. However, when settlers realized that these creatures were edible, the turtles were almost completely exterminated. From 1968 to 1978, Bermudian environmentalists flew thousands of green turtle eggs to the area from Costa Rica and buried them on various beaches. Sea turtles return to lay eggs on the beach where they were born, so scientists hoped that the hatchlings would one day lay new eggs in Bermuda.

Initial signs that this mission had been successful were discovered in 2015. For the first time in almost 100 years, green turtles were naturally born in Bermuda. Scientists counted 90 hatched eggs.

The Bermuda Turtle Project continues the work of studying sea turtles in order to better contribute to their conservation. The group has tagged more than 3,500 green turtles, tracking their movements through the ocean.

Green turtles are protected by Bermuda's laws, but they are still threatened by ocean pollution. They are often killed by plastics and gases that get caught in their stomachs.

Bermudians consider it to be a sign of spring because it tends to arrive with the warmer weather. When two longtails are courting, they fly right next to each other so that their long tail feathers brush against each other. Longtails make their nests in cracks and openings along seaside cliffs and rocks. They lay one egg and nest from April to June. The fluffy chicks are raised in the nest during the summer and are fed with fish and squid caught at sea.

In recent years, the longtail population has declined due to a combination of factors such as coastline development and water pollution. Global warming has also made the sea level rise, flooding some of the longtails' nests. To help this important bird, in 1997 the Bermudians invented an alternative kind of nest for the longtails. These "igloos" are made out of Styrofoam and cement. They are strong but light and provide good protection for the birds from the sun. Longtails happily nest in these artificial homes, and they can be installed on clifftops, terraces, or sea walls in areas free from predators like dogs and cats.

NONSUCH ISLAND

Bermuda's Nonsuch Island was named by an English group that declared "nonesuch was ever its equal." The island is a nature reserve that is closed to the public except for occasional educational tours. Strict visitor limits protect the island as the home of Bermuda's most threatened species. These include the cahow, also called the Bermuda petrel.

The cahow, which only ever nests in Bermuda, had seemingly disappeared from the islands in the 1600s. Stories say that in the early 1500s, Spanish conquistadors heard the cahows shrieking their loud courtship calls and believed they were a sign of evil spirits. As a result, many sailors referred to Bermuda as the "Isle of Devils." There were a million of these birds flying about Bermuda at the time. However, between the hogs already living on the island and the arrival of the British settlers, plus the cats and dogs that came with them, much of the cahow population had been eaten by 1621 and was soon after considered extinct.

Because of this, it was a shock when a small colony of cahows was found in 1951 by a team of scientists in Bermuda. The team found seven nests. One

of the assistants on that journey was 15-year-old David Wingate. Wingate was so thrilled with the discovery that he decided to dedicate the rest of his life to protecting cahows and their island home.

Wingate went on to become Bermuda's first conservation officer in 1962. He launched a large-scale ecological restoration project on Nonsuch Island aimed at recreating the kind of environment that existed in Bermuda before the arrival of humans. When Wingate began his project, Nonsuch Island was full of feral goats and rats. It took years to take out foreign plants and animals and replace them with native and endemic species. Four important species that were wiped out in the 1600s have been successfully reintroduced since the project was undertaken: the yellow-crowned night heron, the West Indian topshell, the land hermit crab, and the cahow.

Encouraging cahows to nest on the island took some creativity. Cahows are instinctive burrowers and dig a hole in the soil when it is time to nest. The presence of predators and human structures have challenged this natural nesting activity, so Wingate devised an artificial burrow. Originally made from unwieldy cement, the artificial burrows are now designed from durable plastic with a long tunnel and a dark nest chamber that mimics the construction of a natural burrow. A cahow lays one egg in a nesting season and returns to its burrow every night until the egg hatches in June. From the 1951 search that found 7 breeding pairs, there are now about 100 nesting pairs of cahows that live on Nonsuch Island. In 2003, the cahow reclaimed its position as the national bird of Bermuda.

INTERNET LINKS

www.bios.edu
The Bermuda Institute of Ocean Studies is a research organization based out of Bermuda that explores ocean life and tracks the effects of climate change and pollution in marine habitats.

www.kbb.bm
Keep Bermuda Beautiful organizes clean-ups and educational programs to keep Bermuda healthy, clean, and beautiful.

www.livingreefs.org
Living Reefs is an organization that encourages local coral reef restoration and replanting in Bermuda.

www.nonsuchisland.com/live-cahow-cam/
Depending on the time of year, you can get a close-up look at life inside a cahow burrow through this livestream of the "Cahow Cam" on Nonsuch Island.

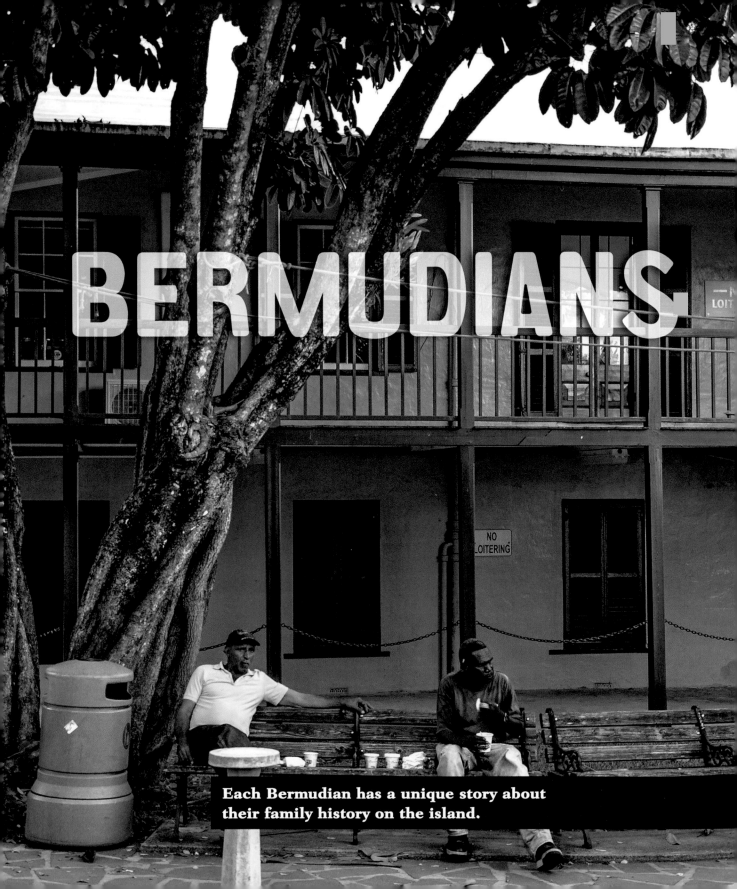

BERMUDIANS

Each Bermudian has a unique story about their family history on the island.

BERMUDA'S PEOPLE REFLECT THE history of the island as a British colony and as a foothold of the slave trade. Black Bermudians can often trace their history to enslaved or free islanders from the Caribbean, and a smaller number came directly from Africa. Overall, Bermudians have a mixed ancestry with British, Caribbean, Native American, and Portuguese roots.

Black Bermudians have made up the majority of residents in Bermuda since the late 18th century. Today, they compose about 52 percent of the population. White Bermudians represent about 31 percent of islanders. About 9 percent are mixed race, 4 percent are Asian, and 4 percent identify as "other."

With a population of 63,908 people in 2019, Bermudians have many stories to tell about their heritage. About two-thirds of the people living in Bermuda today are "Onions" or real Bermudians (at least one parent is Bermudian). The rest are international citizens living and working in Bermuda.

NATIVE AMERICAN HERITAGE

The first Native Americans came to Bermuda from Connecticut. There was a war between the Pequot people and British settlers over the death

"Just enjoy life
while you're
alive. Enjoy the
sunshine, the
flowers, and birds."
–Johnny Barnes

of a Boston trader. This war sparked the destruction of the tribe's villages by colonists. Many Native Americans died in the fight, and those who survived were captured and enslaved.

Many Pequot captives were taken to Bermuda and sold at St. George's Square. Over the following decades, Native Americans from other groups were sold in Bermuda as well. In general, Native Americans were treated very poorly on the island. Many enslaved Native Americans were isolated in two villages within St. David's. After emancipation, they developed a sense of privacy and cultural independence there. They survived mainly by fishing and farming. The majority of St. David's residents today are descended from this Native American community.

The group has often been referred to as "Mohawks" or "Mo's" locally. However, it is unlikely that they are actually descended from the Mohawk people. Instead, most have a Pequot, Narragansett, Mohican, or Wampanoag lineage.

St. Clair "Brinky" Tucker helped found a group that is now called the St. David's Islanders and Native Community (SDINC). Tucker is a descendant of the Pequot and Wampanoag peoples. He helped form the group in order to build community, increase pride, raise awareness, and share knowledge about Bermuda's Native American heritage.

In 2002, members of this community held their first-ever event called the "Reconnection Indian Festival." Native Americans from the United States traveled to the island to participate. The event included prayers, storytelling, drumming, and dancing to honor ancestors and share connections. The festival is now being held every two years.

PORTUGUESE HERITAGE

Another group of people who have influenced the history, language, cuisine, and culture of Bermuda are the Portuguese. They are the island's largest ethnic minority group. A large wave of Portuguese immigrants arrived in the mid-1800s. They were recruited from the islands of the Azores, Cape Verde, and Madeira to come to Bermuda as skilled farm workers. Slavery had been abolished in 1834, and Bermuda was searching for low-cost laborers. In

Johnny Barnes was an icon in Bermuda. Every morning from 3:40 a.m. to 10 a.m., white-bearded Barnes stood at a roundabout in Hamilton and waved to people walking, cycling, and driving by. The retired bus driver completed this routine each day, regardless of the weather. Barnes passed away in 2016 at age 93, but he is still remembered for the greetings he shared with neighbors, wandering tourists, schoolchildren, rushing professionals, and everyone in between from 1986 to 2015.

Barnes was labeled the "Friendliest Man in Bermuda," "Mr. Happy Man," and "Mr. Feel Good." His status as a national treasure was confirmed when his image was reproduced in a bronze statue. The statue now stands at the roundabout where Barnes delivered his morning greetings. There's also a portrait

The Johnny Barnes statue was crafted by sculptor Desmond Fountain while Barnes was still living.

of Barnes hung in Bermuda's Visitors Information Center. Barnes was the subject of two short documentary films: Mr. Happy Man *(2012) and* Welcoming Arms *(2015).*

November 1849, the ship *Golden Rule* arrived in Bermuda with 58 Portuguese immigrants from Madeira: 7 children, 16 women, and 35 men.

Over the rest of the 19th century, Portuguese immigrants continued to travel to Bermuda to work in agriculture. They made the growing onion trade possible and shared their knowledge of successful agricultural techniques from their home islands, which were similar to Bermuda in climate. As the focus of

Bermuda's economy shifted from agriculture to tourism, the Portuguese tried to adjust to the change. They suffered from social discrimination and immigration laws that targeted their community in the 20th century. Nevertheless, they continued to make valuable contributions and strengthened their identity through cultural clubs and gatherings. Today, pride in Portuguese heritage is demonstrated in family and community traditions and delicious recipes passed down through generations. People with Portuguese ethnicity represent around 20 percent of the population of Bermuda.

CELEBRATING BLACK HISTORY

Black Bermudians have played an essential role in shaping Bermuda's history. From the earliest experiences of Venturilla, Black men and women have been central figures in Bermuda's developments. They have driven major changes to Bermuda's social, cultural, political, and economic structures.

Emancipation reached Bermuda 30 years before enslaved African Americans were freed. This difference was made abundantly clear in 1835,

Many Black Bermudians were laid to rest in the separate burial grounds for free and enslaved Black people at St. Peter's Church until the churchyard closed in 1854.

when the American ship *Enterprise* was blown off course on its way from Virginia to South Carolina. The ship docked in Bermuda to make repairs and buy supplies. Local customs officials saw the 78 enslaved passengers on board and prevented the ship from leaving Bermuda. First, the governor would have to rule on whether these people were free or not. After hearing testimony from all of the enslaved passengers, the governor gave them a choice to stay in Bermuda as free citizens or continue on their journey back to the United States. All but one family of six chose to stay. Today, many Bermudians can trace their lineage back to those 72 passengers.

To honor the importance of the Black experience on the islands, the Bermuda African Diaspora Heritage Trail was organized. It is a self-guided tour with 11 stops all over the island that highlight Black history. The trail is also part of the UNESCO Slave Route Project.

On the east end is St. Peter's graveyard, where free and enslaved Black islanders were buried in a segregated area. St. George's Historical Museum, also on the east end, contains the barred cell windows of white missionary John Stephenson. The reverend was imprisoned for six months for illegally preaching to Black and integrated congregations in 1800.

The Bermuda Heritage Museum in St. George tells the story of Sarah "Sally" Bassett, an enslaved woman. In 1730, she was found guilty of attempting to poison her enslavers, Thomas and Sarah Foster. Poisoning was a fairly common form of resistance to slavery at the time. Bassett insisted she was innocent at her trial, but she was convicted of the crime. Her punishment was to be burned to death at the eastern end of Hamilton Harbour. According to folklore, a small purple flower—the Bermudiana—bloomed in her ashes. Bassett was executed on one of Bermuda's hottest days. Even now, a very hot day on the island may be called a "Sally Bassett day."

The Tucker House Museum is also on the east end. It is the site of the Joseph Rainey Memorial Room, where visitors can see copies of speeches Joseph Hayne Rainey made during his term in the U.S. House of Representatives. Rainey was enslaved from birth in South Carolina, but his father purchased his family's freedom when Rainey was 14. Rainey was drafted into the Confederate Army during the Civil War, but he managed to escape from a blockade-running

In the past, famous faces seen around Bermuda included the singer David Bowie and his wife, Iman. The first supermodel, Twiggy, was another visitor from Great Britain. Film stars Michael Douglas and Catherine Zeta-Jones have a home on the island. Douglas has been coming to the island since he was a child. His mother, Diana Dill, was born in Bermuda.

Famous Bermudians include a number of well-known athletes, writers, artists, and scientists. Gina Swanson, who was crowned Miss World in 1979, hails from Bermuda. So does Shiona Turini, a stylist and costume designer now based in the United States. Turini has designed wardrobes for the show Insecure *and the film* Queen & Slim. *In 2019, Turini proudly served as the grand marshal for the Bermuda Day Parade in her home country.*

Bermuda's Shiona Turini *(front left)* has made a name for herself in the global fashion industry.

ship to Bermuda. He spent his time on the island working as a barber until the war ended. Rainey returned to South Carolina and became the first African American to serve in the U.S. House of Representatives in 1870. He was reelected four times and used his terms to advocate desegregation and equal rights.

On the west end of the tour is Cobb's Hill Wesleyan Methodist Church, the first organized church for free Black and enslaved people on the island. It was built by and for Black Bermudians. The community worked mainly by candlelight in the evening after their daily work was finished. The church was dedicated in 1827.

Two other stops on the tour are the Commissioner's House at the National Museum of Bermuda and the Royal Naval Dockyard. The museum includes artifacts like iron slave restraints. The dockyard is included because free Black and enslaved Bermudians worked to build the naval base.

BRITISH HERITAGE

The iconic British red phone box is not only found in Great Britain. It is also a staple for photo opportunities in Bermuda.

As a British Overseas Territory of the United Kingdom, Bermuda is politically tied to the United Kingdom. More than that, Bermudians retain and celebrate their British cultural connections and have worked to keep the relationship strong. The influence of England can be found throughout the island. British accents, tea time, red phone boxes, driving on the left, and a formal style of dress and manners are all nods to British customs. Many Bermudians attend university or travel in the United Kingdom to celebrate and learn about their common heritage.

INTERNET LINKS

bermudianheritagemuseum.com
Exhibits and articles about the multicultural heritage of Bermuda can be found on the Bermudian Heritage Museum website.

bernews.com/bermuda-profiles/
Find out more about the Bermudian men and women whose lives changed history.

LIFESTYLE

Life in Bermuda is colorful, from the brilliant hues of the natural landscape to the cheerful pastel paint on houses.

7

LIFESTYLE IN BERMUDA IS influenced by heritage, the tourist and business economy, and the high standard of living on the island. Life in Bermuda is generally more formal, especially in terms of clothing and manners, than in its nearest neighbor, the United States. Even the stereotypical Bermuda shorts are worn in a prescribed fashion. Bermudians are well educated and attend schools on and off the island. The high standard of living is also accompanied by high costs for housing and imported goods like groceries, gas, and other household items. These factors all play into daily life for Bermudians and temporary residents of the islands.

"The short pant is a terrible fashion choice. Unless it is from Bermuda."
—Winston Churchill

A FASHION STATEMENT

Most Bermudians follow the clothing trends of large cities in the United States and the United Kingdom. Smart casual is the most common style of

Bermuda legalized same-sex marriage in 2018 and hosted its first LGBTQ Pride parade in 2019.

dress today at restaurants and around town. It is casual with an added touch of modesty; the Bermuda Tourism Authority describes it as "British-meets-the-beach." Women's clothing tends toward colorful or patterned skirts and dresses. Men dining out will stick with button-up shirts.

One of the most unusual styles is the island's famous Bermuda shorts. They were first worn long ago when the British army was sent to India. Because of the hot temperatures there, soldiers were issued shorts as part of their gear. By the 1920s and 1930s, these same shorts had become available to the general public.

This fashion trend was enthusiastically adopted in Bermuda, where the shorts were well-suited to the warm and humid climate. The shorts are worn by nearly everyone in Bermuda—including businessmen on their way to important meetings. A 2000 law even made it possible to wear Bermuda shorts in the House of Assembly.

These shorts can be casual, but when a blazer, dress shirt, and tie are added, they become formal office attire. It is essential that they are made correctly, however. The proper pair of Bermuda shorts ends 3 inches (7.62 cm) above the knee with a 3-inch (7.62 cm) hem. A nice pair of knee socks finishes the look. Women wear Bermuda shorts as well, but they are usually more casual and come in a wider range of colors.

WEDDING TRADITIONS

A little less than half the weddings in Bermuda are between Bermudians. The rest are for tourists who come expressly to get married in such a beautiful place. Unlike some countries, there is no residency requirement for weddings on the islands. In other words, you do not have to live on the islands in order to get married there. Instead, couples, either locals or visitors, are required to give notice of the intended marriage to the local newspaper so it can be published two weeks before the event. Some weddings are held at the Marriage Room of the Registry, while others are held in historic houses, churches, or hotels, or even on the beach. It is traditional for couples to travel to and from the wedding in a horse-drawn carriage with a uniformed driver.

One Bermuda marriage tradition is to have separate cakes for the bride and groom. The bride's cake is usually a fruitcake with several tiers, which represents fertility. On the top is a silver leaf to symbolize purity. The groom's cake is usually rather plain and has a gold leaf on the top to represent wealth. Other couples have a large cake with three levels. One is for the bride, one is for the groom, and the other is for guests. Frequently, the cake is topped with a cedar sapling that is later planted in the yard of the couple's first house.

With more than 100 churches in Bermuda, couples looking for a religious wedding have many options.

AT SCHOOL

In Bermuda, no matter if you go to public or private school, education is controlled by the government. School is mandatory from ages 5 through 16. Primary school is the first six years, middle school is three years, and senior level is four years long.

The Ministry of Education is currently working to improve the public school system in Bermuda through major reforms. With the passage of the Education Amendment Act in 2021, work began to phase out middle schools in favor of a two-tiered system. The reforms have also introduced industry-specific schools for high school seniors that are called Signature Learning Programmes.

Bermuda's schools are responsible for the country's high literacy rate, which is around 98 percent. There are a number of private schools on the island that offer different environments and education styles. The Bermuda High School for Girls is the only non-coeducational school on the island and has been educating girls for more than 125 years. Saltus Grammar School is the largest private school and was founded in 1888. The Warwick Academy—probably the oldest functioning school in the Western Hemisphere since it was founded in 1662—uses a U.K. curriculum, while Mount St. Agnes Academy follows a U.S. model. The Bermuda Institute is a Seventh-day Adventist school and uses a church-based program, while the Somersfield Academy offers a Montessori curriculum for its younger students that is based on learning through play. In recent years, home schools have also been an educational alternative. These small schools meet the specific learning needs of certain children.

Bermuda does not have any universities. It does have a two-year community college called Bermuda College, which was built in 1979. Many young people go abroad for college after finishing high school. Usually, students choose the United States or Canada. Those wanting a law degree commonly head to U.K. universities, as Bermuda's laws are based on the British system.

Any Bermudian who wants to go to college can, even if he or she cannot afford it, thanks to the Bermuda Government's National Education Guarantee Scheme. It was organized in 1994, and it offers students education loans. According to the 2016 census, about 36 percent of Bermudians aged 25 to 64 had earned a university degree.

AT HOME

The typical family in Bermuda rents or owns a home in one of Bermuda's cities. In fact, the entire population of Bermuda is considered urban. Hamilton has the highest number of permanent residents. Some buildings are divided into multi-family dwellings, but you will not see any high-rises. Most houses are small to medium-sized with one or two stories.

You can find many Bermudians at home in small cottages distinguished by their pastel-painted stone walls and tiered white roofs. Although the rows of whitewashed roofs make an appealing postcard image, they are primarily functional. Bermuda's roofs offer a creative solution to the lack of fresh water on the island: They are part of a water catchment system. Homes are constructed with large water tanks built beneath them. This has been a practice since Bermuda's early colonial days, and archaeological sites usually contain a cistern dug near or under a house. Rainwater is collected on the rooftops and funneled through special channels and gutters down into the tank for

Gleaming white roofs atop pink and peach houses are among the most memorable sights in Bermuda, and they serve an essential purpose for life on the islands.

A good system of public transportation connects all nine parishes in Bermuda. The main network is made up of ferries and buses. The bus routes head in two general directions: toward St. George's or toward Somerset. Most Bermudian households also own a car, and some have additional motorcycles or scooters for getting around.

The Bermuda Railway, nicknamed "Old Rattle and Shake," operated across the island from 1931 to 1948. The line traveled from Somerset to St. George's, but laying the tracks was a costly venture involving the construction of many bridges and tunnels. A 1908 ban on automobiles in Bermuda was lifted in 1946, and cars started popping up on the island. The costs of maintaining the railway soon seemed unnecessary. The old tracks were refashioned into a bicycle and pedestrian trail in the 1980s. Many Bermudians use the scenic 18-mile (29 km) path for slower travel or recreation.

Four ferry lines and multiple roads connect the parts of Bermuda. During the summer, buses and ferries often become crowded with tourists bound for the beach.

later use. Because the water starts on the roof, it is essential that the surface is kept as white and clean as possible. The rainwater is also disinfected with bleach before being used as drinking water. You might hear Bermudians call a rainy day a "good day for the tank."

The roofs are made from limestone slates processed from quarries on the island. The slates are mortared together in a stepped arrangement to help the water run off the roof and into the collection tank. The limestone is also more resistant to hurricane winds and tropical storms than other materials. Roofs are whitewashed regularly for maximum cleanliness.

STAYING HEALTHY

In addition to a high standard of living, Bermuda also has high health standards. According to the World Bank, the life expectancy in 2019 was 81 years old. The country also has a low infant mortality rate, and it experienced no maternal deaths in 2020. However, about 75 percent of adults are considered overweight or obese, and many have chronic illnesses related to this condition. Bermuda's Ministry of Health aims to provide affordable and effective health systems to enhance well-being on the islands. Special services are provided for the elderly and people with disabilities.

During the COVID-19 pandemic, Bermuda responded quickly with public health guidance. From January 2020 to June 2021, there were 2,499 confirmed cased of the virus and 33 deaths in Bermuda. The government's vaccine strategy was put into action in January 2021, and by June more than 73,000 doses had been administered. Key partners in Bermuda's approach to health are the Ministry of Health and the Bermuda Health Council.

Dr. Barbara Ball was the first Bermudian-born female doctor. She began practicing medicine in Bermuda in 1954.

INTERNET LINKS

www.bermudarailway.net
Find information about the old Bermuda Railway and the current trail on this website researched and created by author Simon Horn.

www.college.bm
Visit the website of Bermuda College to learn about opportunities in higher education in Bermuda.

RELIGION

St. Peter's Church, Their Majesties Chappell, was established just after the start of the Bermuda colony.

With more than
110 churches,
Bermuda has an
average of about
5 churches per
1 square mile
(2.5 sq km).

8

RELIGIOUS PRACTICE IS AN important part of life for many Bermudians. This is evident in the existence of more than 100 places of worship in Bermuda. Most Bermudians, about 46 percent, worship in Protestant churches. The largest Protestant group is Anglican, representing 15.8 percent of the population according to the 2010 census. The archbishop of Canterbury in England is the main religious figure, followed by the Bishop of Bermuda, who is the head of the Anglican Cathedral in Hamilton. After Protestants, the second largest group are Roman Catholics at 14.5 percent.

Other Protestant churches include African Methodist Episcopal at 8.6 percent and Seventh-day Adventists at 6.7 percent. Pentecostal, Methodist, Presbyterian, Church of God, Baptist, Salvation Army, Brethren, and other Protestant groups are found in smaller numbers on the island. About 9 percent of Bermudians belong to other Christian faiths, and 1 percent are Muslim. A small portion follow folk religions, and less than 1 percent are Jewish or Hindu. Those who do not follow a faith tradition represent 17.8 percent of the country.

BERMUDA'S CHURCHES

Among the many churches found in Bermuda, three stand out as the most unique. The Bermuda Cathedral, also known as the Cathedral of the Most Holy Trinity, is in Hamilton. Its sanctuary burned down in 1884. Two years later, Scottish architect William Hay was hired to rebuild the church. He designed a Gothic-style structure; construction began in 1886 and was completed in 1905. Much of the structure was made with limestone, although some of the stone features were imported from France. The choir stalls and bishop's throne were made of English oak, and the entire church is topped with a copper roof that stands out against the typical white roofs of people's cottages. The angel stained-glass window on the east wall was created by Bermudian artist Vivienne Gilmore Gardner. For those who take the time to climb the 155 steps of the church tower, a beautiful view of Hamilton and the ocean can be seen.

The cornerstone of the Bermuda Cathedral dates to 1844, but most of the structure was rebuilt after 1886.

St. Peter's Church is in the town of St. George and is believed to be the oldest continually used Anglican church in the Western Hemisphere. It was first built with Bermuda cedar and a roof made out of palmetto leaves in 1612. Since then, it has been updated, including the addition of a steeple. The altar was built from red cedar in 1615 by the first governor, Richard Moore. The font is roughly 900 years old. It was brought to Bermuda by some of the very first settlers. Outside the church are two graveyards—one set aside for Black people and the other for white people. The grave of Sir Richard Sharples is found there as well, along with a 500-year-old cedar tree.

The Unfinished Church is on Church Folly Lane in St. George's. Work began on the structure in 1874 but was abandoned after financial shortages, arguments with the Anglican community, and several severe storms during construction. The government has been restoring the church so that it can be used for public tours and even as a venue for cultural performances.

The elements of the Bermuda Cathedral come together to create a truly multicultural masterpiece with Scottish, French, English, and Bermudian influences.

The open arches of the Unfinished Church create a dramatic backdrop for photos and weddings.

MINORITY RELIGIONS

Bermuda also has small Muslim and Jewish communities. According to the Masjid Muhammad Mosque located in Hamilton, there are about 600 Muslims in Bermuda. Practicing Muslims are thought to have first worshipped in Bermuda in 1975. In addition to the mosque, Bermuda's Muslim community also supports Muslim elementary students at the Clara Muhammad School.

From 1694 until 1760, laws prohibited Jews from doing business in Bermuda. This unwelcoming environment for Jews meant that the country did not develop a substantial Jewish community until much later. During World War II, U.S. soldiers on base in Bermuda practiced their Jewish faith and invited Jewish islanders to join them. This arrangement continued until the U.S. Navy closed the base in 1994. Since then, the Jewish Community of Bermuda has been established in Pembroke. The community has about 120 members today. They meet in a sanctuary and celebrate holidays together at the Bermuda Jewish Community Center.

Bermuda has a reputation for being charitable. This community-centered spirit can be traced back to the Friendly Societies of the 1800s. Many Bermudians say their instinct toward generosity is rooted in their religious beliefs. When an international disaster occurs, such as the Asian tsunami of 2004 or hurricanes near Atlantic islands, Bermuda has been there to offer money and other resources to help.

Faith inspires some Bermudians to volunteer in their community through local and international organizations. Some give their free time to Habitat for Humanity, which has been building and restoring affordable homes on the islands since 2000. The Red Cross has operated in Bermuda since 1950 and relies on volunteers for blood donations and a task force of responders when a disaster strikes. Volunteers also assist with the Coalition for the Protection of Children, which is dedicated to making childhood in Bermuda safer and healthier.

INTERNET LINKS

jewishbermuda.com
The Jewish Community of Bermuda hosts community events and worships together in Pembroke, Bermuda.

stpaulamechurchbermuda.org
Learn about St. Paul African Methodist Episcopal Church, the first church built by and for Black Bermudians.

www.masjidmuhammad.net
Visit the website of the Masjid Muhammad Mosque and Muslim community in Bermuda.

www.stpeters.bm
The St. Peter's Church website describes its history as one of the oldest Anglican churches and contains information about the segregated cemeteries in its churchyard.

LANGUAGE

Long Story Short is a bookstore in St. George's specializing in works by Black and female authors.

9

BERMUDA IS A BRITISH TERRITORY, but it is an arena for many languages beyond English to be spoken and celebrated. Standard English is the language used in schools, government offices, and professional settings in written and spoken form. Written English follows the British spelling system. However, many Bermudians will easily switch from standard English in a professional setting to Bermudian English in casual settings. Bermudian English combines many influences of Bermuda's heritage into a unique spoken dialect.

The Bermudian accent seems to mix British and American pronunciations, and some might detect an occasional Caribbean cadence. It is common to hear the English accent, but American, Jamaican, Canadian, French, and many other accents are also in play.

You might catch Portuguese words being exchanged. Portuguese is considered Bermuda's second language thanks to the many immigrants from the Azores, Madeira, and Cape Verde who settled in the country. It

Tourists bring a variety of languages and accents to Bermuda every day.

is often used in public buildings, museums, newspaper ads, signs, menus, and ATMs in Bermuda. Caribbean dialects are fairly common, too. Between the migration of people to Bermuda to live or work and the large seasonal flux of tourists, many different words, phrases, accents, and languages can make their way into daily conversation.

NEWS AND BROADCASTING

Six days a week, the people of Bermuda read their only daily newspaper, the *Royal Gazette*. It was founded in 1828 and has a circulation of 30,000. In 1997, the newspaper went online, and now about 20,000 people visit the website each day. *Bernews* is another online news provider. It was launched in 2010 and became the only media outlet with round-the-clock coverage. The *Worker's Voice* is published several times a year by the Bermuda Industrial

Here are some examples of words and expressions used by the people of Bermuda:

Bermudian	Standard English
ace boy/ace girl	*best friend*
Bermy	*Bermuda*
bring your blinds	*bring your sunglasses*
Chingas!	*Wow!*
cool-cool	*I'm fine*
the rock	*Bermuda*
greeze	*a large meal*
horse	*moped/motorcycle*
I'll be there Bermuda time.	*I'll be late.*
Onions	*born-and-bred Bermudians*
Piggly Wiggly	*grocery store*
session	*a party*
Wopnin?	*What's happening?*

Another sound you might catch is the reversal of v *and* w. *This dates back to the way the English settlers of the 17th century spoke. "Words" might be pronounced "vords," and "value" becomes "walue."*

Union. Newspapers from the United States, along with those from Canada and Britain, are also available.

Radio broadcasting first began in Bermuda in 1946 with the Bermuda Broadcasting Company (BBC). Radio talk shows are quite popular. Music stations are required to include "local content," meaning that they have to feature at least two locally sung or locally orchestrated songs per hour. There are 13 radio stations currently operating.

The BBC branched out to provide television programming starting in 1958. Today, the BBC operates two television stations that are affiliates of ABC and CBS. In 2007, a government information television station called CITV was launched. It was designed to send out messages directly from government officials to the people. CITV is also now available for livestreaming

The BBC (not to be confused with the British Broadcasting Company) is the largest broadcaster in Bermuda.

Polite greetings are expected between friends and strangers when meeting in public places in Bermuda.

on the internet. Many homes and hotels have satellite and cable television subscriptions. Streaming services can also be accessed online.

FORMALITIES

Bermudians are very polite people and hold firmly to the traditional English idea of good manners. Everyone greets one another with a very proper "Good morning!" and "Good afternoon!" before starting any conversation, buying a product in a store, or any other interaction. Handshakes are standard in many interactions, especially between men. Bermudians are generally known as a friendly group of people.

NATIONAL LIBRARY

Bermuda's National Library was founded in 1839. The governor at the time, William Reid, championed its creation. The library was first set up in what is now the Cabinet Building in Hamilton. It started with a humble collection of 276 books. In 1917, it moved its materials to its present location of Par-la-ville in Hamilton. The library has grown to contain more than 115,300 volumes today. The current library building also houses the museum collection of the Bermuda Historical Society.

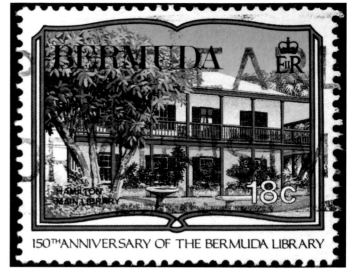

The Bermuda Library celebrated its 150th anniversary in 1989 with a commemorative stamp.

INTERNET LINKS

bernews.com
Bernews is Bermuda's main online news source with a steady stream of headlines.

www.bnl.bm
The Bermuda National Library website is a trove of information with links to many important Bermudian resources.

www.royalgazette.com
Check out the latest reporting from Bermuda's trusted publication, the *Royal Gazette*.

John Stephens was Bermuda's first National Librarian. He served in that role from 1839 until 1853.

ARTS

FRASER FAMILY WING

masterworks
Museum of Bermuda Art

The Masterworks Museum highlights artwork inspired
by Bermudian scenes or made by Bermudian artists.

10

BERMUDA'S COLORFUL SUNSETS, breathtaking scenery, and exciting history have stimulated creative art for centuries. News of the *Sea Venture*'s shipwreck in 1609 is said to have inspired William Shakespeare to write his play *The Tempest*. It is the story of Europeans marooned on a strange island. Tales of daring and adventure alongside descriptions of Bermuda's natural wonders have drawn outside artists and writers to its shores throughout its history. In addition, Bermuda has produced architecture, music, dance, crafts, and fine art with its own unique signature to share with the world.

Shakespeare's play *The Tempest* references the Bermuda islands, calling them "the still-vex'd Bermoothes."

ARCHITECTURE

Although Bermuda's artists and authors abound, one of the main canvases for Bermudian art is the architecture of the islands. Bermuda's homes, traditionally pink, are considered to be the only real indigenous art form on the islands. These little pink cottages are distinctive and grace many different postcards and prints for tourists.

Traditional homes are built with Bermuda limestone. For 350 years, it was the only building material available. The stone is a combination of sand packed tightly with a small amount of crushed coral and seashells, and it is sourced from Bermuda's quarries. It is cut into oblong building blocks that are quite strong but also absorbent to help with the island's humidity. They are mortared together and painted with whitewash to seal the cracks. In recent years, concrete has largely replaced the coral rock as a building material.

The homes have small eaves built in to help direct water away from the houses when the occasional tropical storm strikes. High tray ceilings improve air flow inside the houses to keep things cool. Top-hinged window shutters offer protection from sun, wind, and rain.

Grander homes were built in a variety of European- and American-inspired styles through Bermuda's history. The 18th-century influence of English Georgian mansions is apparent in the preference for symmetry around the island. Verdmont in Smith's Parish, constructed at the turn of the 18th century, was built on the cusp of this style and also borrows from architectural practices of the American South. The structure of Verdmont itself is like a time capsule, largely unchanged for 300 years.

In the backyards of some Bermuda homes are odd-looking structures known as butteries. The traditional buttery dates to days before refrigerators and ice were imported. Back then, Bermudians needed a way to keep their butter, milk, and food cool, and a buttery provided the right environment. Butteries usually have a brick staircase leading up to the entrance and a high pointed roof. Today, these buildings are used for everything from studio apartments to tool sheds or beach houses.

MOONGATES

Another unusual type of architecture found in Bermuda is the moongate. Originally from Asia, these sculptures are usually made out of coral blocks in a standing semicircle. They first came to the island in 1830 when a sea captain

brought a plan with him based on structures he had seen in a Chinese garden. He designed the pattern himself and then proceeded to build it. It was a success, and soon Bermudians were copying the idea for their gardens and homes. While those in Chinese gardens are made out of wood, Bermuda uses stone.

Moongates are often placed into garden walls or set against a seaside view. Bermudians believe that if a couple walks through the moongate while holding hands, they are guaranteed everlasting happiness and good luck throughout their marriage. Locals and tourists alike exchange their wedding vows in front of a moongate to bring good fortune. There is even a song dedicated to the structure called "Step Through a Moongate" that was recorded by Ralph Blane in 1983.

Moongates are difficult to construct and make use of a wooden template that is removed once all the stones are in place.

"BERMUDA IS ANOTHER WORLD"

Hubert Smith and the Coral Islanders performed this song (written by Smith):

"Bermuda is another world—700 miles at sea
And the way people greet you is like a friendly melody.
To touch a flower in the morning, to listen to a honeybee,
To hear a bird who sings a song just to say that he is free.
Bermuda is another world, turn around, I'll tell you why
Just to watch the morning sunrise, from the sea up to the sky.
Look across the Harbor, see the multicolored sails
To water ski on the water that always leaves a snowy trail.
Bermuda is another world, turn around and you'll be gone,
But there will always be a memory that will linger on and on.
And someday I'll hear you say, just as I say today . . .
Bermuda is another world!"

ISLAND SOUNDS

Music in Bermuda has strong international influences that are delivered with a Bermudian twist. The music heard around Bermuda is often a combination of calypso and steel pan. Musical traditions from Jamaica, Puerto Rico, and Trinidad seem at home in this setting. Jazz is another major style in Bermuda. It has produced world-famous jazz artists, such as Lance Hayward and Alan Silva.

Balladeers like Hubert Smith have written lyrical and sometimes humorous odes to Bermudian life. Smith's song "Bermuda Is Another World" from 1969 is a favorite anthem of the island. Smith performed it for tourists, royal visitors, and dignitaries many times during his career.

The funk band The Invaders exploded onto the world music scene from Bermuda in the 1970s. Contemporary musicians from Bermuda include reggae artists Collie Buddz and Mishka. Singer-songwriter Heather Nova and performer Aisha Davis are also Bermudians.

Bermuda also has a musical surprise: bagpipes. It is a surprising sound in the subtropical climate, but it originates from the Scottish and Canadian regiments of the British army that were sent to Bermuda in the 18th and 19th centuries. The bagpipe music was played regularly by the troops, and after a while it became a tradition.

In 1992, the Bermuda Islands Pipe Band joined together two existing bagpipe bands. It performs at different ceremonies for small groups, at hotels, and at weddings. Local events like Remembrance Day and the Beating the Retreat ceremonies are usually accompanied by the pipe and drum music. It has also performed overseas in the United States, Canada, Scotland, and Germany. The 20-member band of pipers and drummers wears kilts in the traditional Gordan tartan.

GOMBEY TRADITION

The most popular and well-known folk artists in Bermuda are the Gombey (GOM-bay) dancers. They dance to the West African tribal music of kettle and snare drums and whistles while wearing masks, capes, and peacock feathers and holding bows, arrows, and tomahawks. Their dances often convey stories that are based on a combination of Christian Bible tales, British history, and Native American culture. The dancers are almost always male, and fathers teach sons how to dance. Their costumes are amazingly colorful, with long hats made with tropical bird feathers, usually peacock. Some costumes are decorated with tiny mirrors or are resplendent with ribbons. The dancers' faces and bodies are completely covered up with the costumes. Gombey dancers use wooden sticks to play snare drums. This part of the tradition is borrowed from British military parades.

Collie Buddz (*right*) broke into the international music industry with reggae songs like "Come Around" and "Blind to You."

Gombey dancers cannot be missed as they stomp down the street in parades or perform on holidays and in hotels.

At one point, Gombey dancing was outlawed in Bermuda. The only allowed dances were on Christmas Day and Boxing Day. Wearing masks helped the dancers protect their identity as they celebrated their African, Native American, and Bermudian heritage. Once the strict rules around Gombey were relaxed, forming troupes of dancers was an excellent way to bring neighborhoods and families together and celebrate pride in Black Bermudian identity.

The word "Gombey" is derived from the name of a certain African drum and means "rhythm" in the Bantu language. As Gombey dancers perform, they begin to speed up and become more uninhibited. People often join in the dancing from the sidelines.

WRITERS AT WORK

Over the years, a number of famous writers have come to Bermuda to visit, write, and relax. They include: Thomas Moore, Eugene O'Neill, James Thurber, Sinclair Lewis, Noel Coward, Rudyard Kipling, Frances Hodgson Burnett, Edna Ferber, Ian Fleming, E. B. White, C. S. Forester, and Peter Benchley. Stories from Bermuda were published in Mark Twain's first book *Innocents Abroad* in 1869. Twain returned to write about Bermuda for articles in the *Atlantic Monthly* magazine in 1877 and 1878. Later, he regularly visited the island for pleasure or to improve his health.

Mark Twain traveled to Bermuda on steamships eight times between 1867 and his death in 1910.

In addition to visiting writers, there are many works by Bermudian writers. Every five to six years, the government of Bermuda awards literary prizes for exceptional contributions to Bermuda's literary culture in poetry, fiction, nonfiction, and drama. Paul Maddern is a Bermudian poet who has twice won the Bermuda Government Literary Award for his poetry collections. His most recent publication is *The Tipping Line* from 2018. *Girlcott* by Florenz Webbe Maxwell won the prize for Children's and Young Adult Fiction in 2018. It tells the story of a 16-year-old girl who becomes involved in Bermuda's Theatre Boycott of 1959.

Another of Bermuda's contemporary authors is John Cox. Born in Bermuda in 1955, he grew up in a supposedly haunted house built by his distant relative, Captain William Cox, in 1802. After attending college in Canada and the United States, Cox returned to Bermuda and began writing articles for *Bermudian Magazine*, a publication that covers cultural news and stories on the art and people of Bermuda. Eventually, he became the associate editor. His many books include *Bermuda's Favorite Haunts* and *Bermuda Lore*.

Many other Bermudian writers have focused on recording the history of the island. William S. Zuill and Eva Hodgson are some of the more famous names in Bermuda's nonfiction tradition. Hodgson was a writer and antiracist activist who explored Black history and experiences in Bermuda.

MUSEUMS AND GALLERIES

Most people go to Bermuda to enjoy its natural beauty, but the island also offers interesting museums and historic buildings. Many people stop by The Bermuda Aquarium, Museum & Zoo in Flatts Village, while others head for the Gibbs Hill Lighthouse to see the oldest cast-iron lighthouse in the world. The Bermuda Historical Society Museum in Hamilton was originally the house of Bermuda's first postmaster. The public library is inside, as well as the original letter from George Washington asking for gunpowder during the American Revolution.

In St. George's, the Bermuda National Trust Museum is located inside what was the home of former governor Samuel Day (who served from 1698 to 1700). When his term was over and the new governor tried to move in, authorities were shocked to find that Day had put the title of the house in his name! Today, the house is a UNESCO World Heritage site, indicating that it is a building of outstanding cultural heritage.

The largest museum is the National Museum of Bermuda. It is located inside a fortress that was built in the 19th century by enslaved workers. There are six large halls inside with displays showing everything from shipbuilding to cruise ship history. Visitors can also tour the fortress itself and see the ramparts, gun ports, underground tunnels, and ammunition supplies.

Even though Bermuda is a relatively small country, it has a deep interest in art. The Bermuda Art Centre at the Dockyard showcases the work of some of the nation's most modern artists. Exhibits change every six weeks, and the center hosts workshops. The Royal Naval Dockyard is also home to Bermuda Clayworks, the island's only commercial pottery workshop where stoneware, vessels, and sculptures are made and sold. Another artistic studio at the Dockyard is Glassworks, where customers can watch the entire process of creating handmade art glass. From a lump of molten glass comes a delicate vase or dish. The City Hall & Arts Centre in Hamilton is home to the Bermuda National Gallery, which houses the national art collection. It features past and present works that tell of Bermuda's history and cultural heritage.

Hamilton's newest museum, Masterworks Museum of Bermuda Art, opened in 2008. It contains the works of many painters inspired by Bermuda's people

and landscape. Famous American artists with work featured in the museum include Winslow Homer, Andrew Wyeth, and Georgia O'Keefe.

The Bermuda National Gallery is housed on the second floor of the Hamilton City Hall and Arts Centre.

ARTS AND CRAFTS

Of course, Bermudian artists are also celebrated in local galleries. Alfred Birdsey's watercolor landscapes of Bermuda and his studio can be visited in Paget Parish, where he lived and worked as an artist. Work by the current Bermudian painter Otto Trott is on display in the Masterworks Gallery. A sculpture called *When Voices Rise* by the artist Chesley Trott is a central feature of Wesley Park, and it commemorates the Theatre Boycott of 1959. A giant mural by Graham Foster called *The Hall of History* chronicles Bermuda's past on a 1,000-square-foot (93 sq m) stretch of wall at the Dockyard.

A stroll through one of Bermuda's many markets will show off the nation's variety of handcrafts. Carvings made from Bermuda cedar are popular, as well as pottery, which is often decorated with images of wildlife or marine

Besides its use in shipbuilding and construction, cedar was an important material for carving and woodwork in Bermuda's past. Cabinetmaking was a profitable pursuit in the 17th and 18th centuries. Samuel and Henry Smith, two brothers, produced a variety of cabinets and carved furniture in their workshop with the help of enslaved workers named Nokey and Augustus. Most of Bermuda's masterfully carved cabinets, woodwork, and furniture was produced by enslaved workers.

Cedar paneling, a trend in the 1700s, is exhibited on the interior walls of Verdmont. Cedar was an essential material for decoration and construction.

Carpentry could also be a prosperous field for Black Bermudians after emancipation. John Henry Jackson was a Black carpenter who was born in Bermuda in 1822. A carved side table he crafted was displayed in the Great Exhibition at London's Crystal Palace in 1851. The exhibition celebrated art, science, and technology from around the globe, including Bermuda. The table is currently part of the collection of the Verdmont Historic House.

life. Bermudian miniatures reproduce pastel pink houses with white roofs, and dolls are made out of banana leaves.

FILM AND TV

Bermuda has frequently been used as a filming location. Peter Benchley, author of *Jaws* and other thrillers, was a writer who enjoyed relaxing and working in Bermuda. In 1977, the film version of his story *The Deep* was filmed in Bermuda because that is where he first found the inspiration for his novel. Benchley met diving expert and treasure hunter Teddy Tucker, who took him to the wreck of the *Constellation*, a ship that sank off the coast of Bermuda. The author began thinking about what might happen if a couple on vacation came across such a wreck, and that was the idea behind his book.

Many of the actors in the movie, including Jacqueline Bisset and Nick Nolte, had to learn how to dive for their roles in the movie. Altogether, before the movie was finished, the cast and crew made 9,895 dives and spent 10,780 man hours underneath the surface of the ocean.

In addition to providing the setting for films, since 1997, Bermuda has hosted an annual international film festival. The nine-day festival screens more than 70 films from 20 countries.

Bermuda has also appeared as a television backdrop. A comedy show called *Crunch and Des* was filmed and set in Bermuda in the 1950s. The show was broadcast in America and Canada and enticed viewers to set Bermuda as their next tourist destination. *Adventures of the Sea Hawk* was a Caribbean adventure show from the 1950s that was also filmed in Bermuda. More recently, part of a season of the *The Bachelorette* was filmed in Bermuda in 2012. The islands and surrounding ocean also provided the setting for a PBS series on marine life in 2014.

Maternal Secrets, shot in 2017, was the first movie filmed in Bermuda in 25 years.

INTERNET LINKS

bipb.bm
The Bermuda Islands Pipe Band website can guide you through the band's history and activities in Bermuda.

communityandculture.bm/contributions-awards/bermuda-literary-awards
Learn more about the writers who have been awarded Bermuda's literary awards on the website of the Department of Culture.

masterworksbermuda.org
View some highlights from the Masterworks Museum collection on its website.

LEISURE

The outdoors provide many opportunities for fun and leisure in Bermuda.

11

THE SAME ATTRACTIONS THAT DRAW visitors to Bermuda are also enjoyed by its residents. Anyone who loves snorkeling, scuba diving, spelunking, kitesurfing, boating, and other marine adventures will never be bored in Bermuda. For those who prefer land activities, participating in or watching sports like cricket, tennis, and golf will always provide entertainment.

"You go to heaven if you want to– I'd druther stay here (in Bermuda)."
—Mark Twain

ISLAND OF CHAMPIONS

Bermuda has produced a number of wonderful athletes. Born in 1951, Clyde Best is considered to be the island's best footballer, or soccer player. Between 1969 and 1976, he played for the West Ham United team in England and was one of the first Black players in English football. Best played for several different teams in more than 180 games. In 2004, he was inducted into the Bermuda National Sports Hall of Fame.

Bermuda's athletes have played in the Olympic Games since 1936. They have participated in boxing, cycling, diving, equestrian sports, luge racing, rowing, sailing, swimming, tennis, and the triathlon.

Bermuda has celebrated many notable Olympic firsts. The first Bermudian women to compete in the Olympics were Phyllis Edness and Phyllis Lightbourn (Jones) in 1948. Heavyweight boxer Clarence Hill won a bronze medal for Bermuda during the 1976 Olympics in Montreal. This was the first Olympic medal for Bermuda. At the 2004 Olympics in Athens, Katura Horton-Perinchief became the first Black female diver from Bermuda.

The 2020 Olympic Games were rescheduled for 2021 in Tokyo. At the Tokyo Olympics, Flora Duffy competed in women's triathlon and won Bermuda's first gold medal. With this vctory, Bermuda became the smallest country by population to win an Olympic gold medal in the Summer Games.

OUT AT SEA

Of all the different sports, Bermuda is most known for sailing. For many, competitive sailing is one of the best things about Bermuda.

People come from all over the world to sail in the Newport Bermuda Race. The tradition began more than a century ago in 1906. Three yachtsmen wanted to find out which one of them was the best sailor. They decided that the best way to determine the answer was to race to Bermuda. The three men, along

Competitors leave the start line and begin the Newport Bermuda Race in 2012.

COMPETING AS A PARA ATHLETE

Jessica Lewis began wheelchair racing when she was 13 years old in 2006. Since then, she has participated in many world competitions for her home country, Bermuda. Lewis excels as a sprinter and competes in the 100-, 200-, and 300-meter races. In 2012, she was the first Bermudian to ever compete in the Paralympic Games. She won a historic gold medal at the 2015 Parapan American Games in Toronto and returned to the Paralympics in 2016. At the Parapan American Games in 2019, Lewis won two gold medals and one silver medal in her events. Lewis has also collected a variety of awards in Bermuda, including Most Fascinating Person of 2015 and Female Athlete of the Year for 2019. Smith's goal in 2021 was to bring home a gold medal from the Tokyo Paralympics.

with the editor of *Rudder* magazine, organized a race starting in Gravesend Bay, Massachusetts, and ending at the shores of Bermuda.

In 1907, a dozen sailboats took off for the 635-mile (1,022 km) ocean race. For a couple of years, many sailors loved the race, but by 1910, only two boats entered the contest. The race came to an end in 1923. The editor of *Yachting* magazine fueled interest in it again, and soon 22 contestants set off, this time from New London, Connecticut. From then on, the race has been held every June in even-numbered years, except during World War II and in 2020.

Since 1958, at least 100 boats have joined the sailing event. There have been 45 races since the challenge was created. In the race in 2018, 170 boats competed. The 2020 race was canceled as a result of the COVID-19 pandemic.

It is not an easy race and not one for new sailors to attempt. The current record for the trip stands at 34 hours and 42 minutes, which was set in 2016. The fast-moving, rough current of the Gulf Stream often makes or breaks a sailor's possibility of winning the race.

Almost every year since 1977, there has been a different sailing race held for amateur sailors. More than 100 yachts join in this race as well. In 1991, the boats continued through near-hurricane conditions. In 1999, electronic navigation was allowed in the race, and two yachts with all-female crews entered for the first time.

CRICKET CLUBS

There is no doubt that Bermudians adore the game of cricket. They listen to games on the radio, watch them on television, and read about them in their newspapers. It is a part of their history. The first recorded cricket match in Bermuda was in 1844. It was a match between soldiers from the British army garrison and a team from the Royal Navy. The next year, the Bermuda Cricket Club was formed, and games popped up all over the island. In 1872, Captain J. Moresby of the Royal Navy came up with an idea to celebrate the 40th anniversary of the abolition of slavery. Why not honor it by having a cricket match? This was the event that would eventually grow into the famous Cup Match.

The Cup Match takes place on the Thursday and Friday before the first Monday of August. The two teams that compete are from cricket clubs in St. George's on the east end and Somerset on the west end.

On the two days of the competition, a strange hush falls over Bermuda. Everything shuts down: stores, restaurants, vendors, and hotels. Even bus and taxi services are hard to find. At the same time, this is when Bermudians eat, drink, dance, and cheer for their favorite team. While some locals attend the game, far more sit at home, listening to each play over the radio or watching the match on television. Parks and beaches are often full of picnickers and campers. The Cup Match is a true island tradition.

TRIATHLONS

For the athlete who wants to do it all, there is the Escape to Bermuda Triathlon. The race begins with a 1-mile (1.6 km) swim at the west end. Competitors jump out of high-speed ferries into the Atlantic Ocean and swim to the Royal Naval Dockyard. Upon reaching the dockyard, they scramble to shore and hop on a bicycle for a 24-mile (38.6 km) ride—the length of the Main Island. Once they get from the western tip to the eastern end, they hit the road for a 6-mile (9.6 km) run on trails along the northern coast of St. George's. Finally, they end up at St. George's King's Square. All participants are invited to a beach party for an awards ceremony.

Flora Duffy is a Bermudian champion of the triathlon who has competed since she was seven years old. Duffy took part in the 2008, 2012, 2016, and 2021 Olympics. She was the International Triathlon Union (ITU) World Series World Champion in 2016 and 2017 and set multiple records. In 2018, Duffy created the Flora Fund to support young athletes in Bermuda. Most recently, she won the gold medal—Bermuda's first—at the 2021 Olympic Games in Tokyo in women's triathlon.

DEEP DIVES

For hundreds of years, sailors knew that the reefs surrounding Bermuda were dangerous. Too many times, powerful waves pushed their ships right into these treacherous spots. Eventually, more than 400 ships were wrecked upon the islands' shores. Although this was a hardship for sailors, it has proven to be a boon for tourists and local scuba divers who explore sunken ships. Diverse fish and other marine creatures have made these shipwrecks their home.

There are dozens of wrecks that attract people to the reefs. Four of the most popular wrecks are the *Mary Celeste*, the *Hermes*, the *Pollockshields*, and the *Cristóbal Colón*.

The *Mary Celeste* was a 225-foot (69 m) boat built for speed. It was driven by steam and had a side wheel. It had to be fast because it was designed to run through Union blockades during the Civil War to smuggle guns, ammunition, supplies, and food to the troops in the South. The ship's end came when a local Bermudian sailor was sure he knew the way through the reefs of his homeland—but he was wrong. Legend has it that his last words were, "I know this reef as well as I know my own house." The ship hit the sharp rocks, filled with water, and sank. Today, the paddle wheel is still completely intact and looks like an oceanic Ferris wheel. Scuba divers enjoy the chance to explore a ship with such a rich history.

The *Pollockshields*, on the other hand, was a 323-foot-long (98 m) German supply ship and cargo steamer. It was captured by the British during World War I. The British used the ship for transporting their own supplies until a storm at sea forced it into a reef along Bermuda's south shore. Some sections of the ship are only 20 feet (6 m) under the surface today. The huge boilers,

The Commonwealth is a union of independent nations with ties to the British Crown. Bermuda competes in the Commonwealth Games as one of the United Kingdom's territories.

decking, and prop are the perfect backdrop for many underwater photographs. Since the *Pollockshields* was carrying ammunition when it sunk, divers still find samples of its explosives.

The *Cristóbal Colón*, a Spanish transatlantic luxury liner that crashed into Bermuda's reef in 1936, is the largest shipwreck in the area. At 499 feet (152 m), it had three decks and now lies in 55 feet (17 m) of water. The wreckage of the ship spreads out over 100,000 square feet (9,290 sq meters) of ocean floor.

Unlike the other three ships, the *Hermes* was intentionally sunk by local dive operators who know how much people like to explore underwater wrecks. It was originally a 165-foot (50 m) World War II steel-hulled freighter. The ship arrived in Bermuda in 1984 with engine trouble. When repairs were estimated to be more than the ship was worth, the crew abandoned it and found a new purpose for it. Unlike many of the accidental wrecks around Bermuda, the *Hermes* is completely intact, sitting upright in 80 feet (24 m) of water 1 mile (1.6 km) offshore at Horseshoe Bay. It provides a big playground for divers and snorkelers alike.

There are dozens of sunken ships submerged around Bermuda to explore when snorkeling or scuba diving.

COURTS AND GREENS

Tennis may have originated in England, but it reached incredible popularity in Bermuda. In the late 19th century, a man named Sir Brownlow Gray built the island's first tennis court in Paget Parish. Gray's daughter, Mary, quickly became the island's first female tennis champion in the 1870s. Another tennis enthusiast, Mary Outerbridge, brought the tennis craze to New York in 1874. Today, Bermuda has some of the best tennis facilities in the world and is the site of many important international competitions.

Golf courses are also numerous in Bermuda. They cover about 17 percent of the island and appeal to visitors and residents. Tourists may need some time to adjust to the windy conditions, which are an added challenge to the game. A number of tournaments are held throughout the year. The Bermuda Championship took place at the Port Royal Golf Course in 2019 and 2020 as part of the PGA Tour. American golfer Brian Gay won the 2020 event.

INTERNET LINKS

bermudarace.com
Find facts and statistics about the Newport Bermuda Race here.

www.bermudagolf.org
View information about the PGA Tour in Bermuda and other golf tournaments on the Bermuda Golf Association website.

www.gotobermuda.com/article/beginners-guide-to-cricket-bermuda
Learn about the basics of cricket in this article from the Bermuda Tourism Authority.

www.olympics.bm
Read about Bermuda's top athletes on the Bermuda Olympic Association website.

FESTIVALS

National Heroes Day is one of the newest holidays celebrated in Bermuda.

12

NO MATTER THE TIME OF YEAR, Bermudians find a way to celebrate their rich heritage and their passion for competition, music, dance, and fun. Christian holidays like Easter and Christmas are occasions for public celebration, and so are national holidays that commemorate historic events. Gombey dancers, and the atmosphere of playfulness and energy they bring with them, are a consistent feature in most Bermudian celebrations.

NEW YEAR

New Year's Day celebrations often start the night before, just as in the United States. Different events are held island-wide on that day. Knighthood is awarded to a local resident, and Companion of the British Empire or Order of the British Empire awards are presented to legislators. Instead of a ball drop, New Year's Eve is celebrated in St. George's with an onion drop! The next day, churches across Bermuda offer New Year's Day services, and there are motocross races on the small Coney Island.

Most families in Bermuda have their own recipe for hot cross buns that they pull out at Easter time.

EASTER TIME

Because of the Catholic influence in Bermuda, Lent is an important time. The Tuesday before, the Roman Catholic Church holds a special mass with performances by church choirs and a gathering in the hall next to the cathedral. In the past, mothers often took their children shopping for new clothes to wear. Girls got new dresses with hats and gloves, while boys got white suits and shiny new shoes. Some families continue this tradition today.

For most Bermudians, Good Friday means church services, followed by two things: flying kites and eating codfish cakes. The kite-flying tradition began in Indonesia more than 3,000 years ago when fisherman used leaf kites to hold up their fishing lines out on the ocean. Talk of the tradition was passed through Asia and reached Europe by the 16th century. Finally, it arrived on Bermuda's shores, where they made it part of their Good Friday celebration.

A typical kite is made out of different colors of tissue paper, wood, metal, and string with long, cloth tails. It is usually formed in the shape of a cross. Kites are sent up in the morning and stay up all day. Only an unexpected rain shower brings them back down to the ground.

Some of the kites are so large that it takes several people to get them off the ground. Other kites are designed with glued paper to make a humming or buzzing sound. Kite flying often involves a religious service, live music, lots of games for children, and a performance by Gombey dancers.

National Heroes Day has been celebrated every June since 2008 to honor the greatest figures from Bermuda's history.

BERMUDA DAY

Bermuda Day is typically held on May 24, which is considered in Bermuda to be the first day of spring. It honors Bermuda's English heritage and the birth of Queen Victoria. Initially it was known as Commonwealth Day, but Lord Pitt, a Black member of the Greater London Council, changed it. During the racial unrest of the 1970s, Pitt suggested the holiday as a way to bring all races of Bermuda together in a single celebration. Today, the annual holiday includes the Marathon Derby, a half-marathon in which people run from Somerset or St. George's (on alternating years) to Hamilton, a distance of 13 miles (21 km).

Other events on Bermuda Day include a parade with floats, music from marching bands, politicians giving speeches, and bicycle races. This is also the day that the Bermuda Fitted Dinghy racing season starts. These dinghies are 14 feet (4.3 m) long, with 40-foot (12 m) masts and yards and yards of sails. The crews on these boats are not in for an easy ride. It is a struggle to stay upright in the wind, and it is not unusual for the dinghies to take on a lot of water. To reduce the weight so they will not capsize, members of the crew jump out—or get pushed off. Watching the crews in the boat trying not to sink is often hilarious for the crowd.

HONORING THE QUEEN

Queen Elizabeth II's birthday is celebrated in Britain and Bermuda in June. A formal parade is held in Hamilton, led by the governor and premier. The Royal

The Bermuda International Sand Sculpture Competition attracts artists and spectators every September in Horseshoe Bay. Participants compete in different categories that are broken down based on talent and experience. There's also a family category so that multiple generations can get involved in a group effort. Teams can have up to six people who fill large plots of sand with masterworks. The sculptures are quite creative, and visitors can watch the artists crafting their sand art. Past entries have been themed around current events, works of fiction, plants and animals, island lore, or Bermuda itself.

Bermuda Regiment marches down Front Street with cannons firing, weapons pointed to the sky, and music setting the beat. The governor, donning an ostrich-plumed hat, accepts a salute. Cruise ship passengers line up on deck to watch the festivities, and if a Royal Navy ship happens to be in port, its crew, dressed in the well-known Bermuda shorts, are backed by the Royal Marines band.

SPORTS AND CELEBRATION

Emancipation Day and Somers Day are held at the same time in Bermuda. They focus on the people's favorite sport of all time: cricket. The Bermuda Cricket Club was founded in St. George's in 1845. Royal Navy Captain J. Moresby began this two-day sporting tradition 27 years later, combining the sport with a nod to the emancipation of enslaved peoples in 1834. There is also a brief recognition of Admiral Sir George Somers, but his part is usually lost in the love for cricket.

Cricket is a game that is popular in Britain, as well as many other places. Played with a bat and a ball, it has two teams with 11 members on each side. It involves cricket pitches, wickets, and bowlers. While there are many fans all over the world, Bermudians are among the most passionate. The entire island comes to a halt for two days each summer to watch the cricket games. More than 7,000 people attend the two-day event, and almost everyone else listens to it on the radio.

HARBOUR NIGHTS

From May to September, every Wednesday night is part of Hamilton's Harbour Nights Festival. The typical signs of a Bermudian celebration accompany the night: Gombey dancers, music, delicious food, and large crowds of tourists and locals. Street food is one of the main attractions, and many participants enjoy a fish sandwich as they watch the swirl of color and activity.

REMEMBRANCE DAY

Remembrance Day is held at the 11th hour of the 11th day of the 11th month. As in England, this holiday is a solemn one in Bermuda. It honors the dead and war veterans of the islands. A parade is held on Front Street in Hamilton. At

Front Street in Hamilton is where the Harbour Nights Festival takes place.

exactly 11:00 a.m., a cannon fires to signal one of the most important moments of the whole service—two minutes of silence. The moments of quiet are observed to honor those who died during active service in World War I, World War II, and the Korean War. Veterans march down Front Street proudly displaying their medals.

CHRISTMAS

Christmas in Bermuda is a wild mix of British, American, and Canadian customs. Special seasonal foods are imported, like gingerbread, mince pies, and brandy butter. Even Christmas trees have to be imported from across the sea. Presents are exchanged, lights are strung, and many churches have nativity scenes.

The Christmas Boat Parade is a spectacular event in Bermuda. It takes place about two weeks before Christmas Day. More than 70 watercraft leave the Royal Bermuda Yacht Club and sail past Front Street, around the tip of Hamilton Harbour, and then slowly back to the yacht club. The boats make a chain almost 2 miles (3.2 km) long. There are more than 1,000 people on them, and an estimated 20,000 locals and tourists come out to watch. At the head of the parade is a marine ship with fire hoses spraying water 70 feet (21 m) high into the air. From the harbor, round after round of sparkling fireworks light up the sky.

The day after Christmas, following English tradition, is Boxing Day. The holiday started long ago in England when aristocrats rewarded their servants by giving them boxes full of food and other treats, as well as awarding them the day off from work. In Bermuda, Boxing Day gives people the chance to

Gombey dancers add a dose of fun and liveliness to Boxing Day festivities in Devonshire.

give gifts to the less fortunate. It is also a day spent making and eating treats like cassava pie and turkey. Families often gather together, and some go to see the motocross races at Coney Island or the pony races at the National Equestrian Centre track.

INTERNET LINKS

bermudafestival.org
The Bermuda Festival of Performing Arts was completely virtual in 2021, so many performances are available to view on its website.

communityandculture.bm
The Department of Culture regularly updates its website with news about upcoming events and information about Bermuda's favorite cultural celebrations.

www.bermudachamber.bm
The Bermuda Chamber of Commerce organizes the Harbour Nights street festival.

www.sandcastle.bm
View entries from previous artists in the Bermuda Sand Castle Competition and take advantage of a free tutorial on how to create sand art.

FOOD

Bermuda onions are a large, mild-tasting, white or yellow variety of onion. Their slightly sweet flavor is excellent either cooked into dishes or raw in salads and sandwiches.

13

BERMUDA'S HISTORY AS A MARITIME and agricultural society has shaped the culinary heritage of the nation. As a maritime center, seafood and local catches of spiny lobster, crab, oysters, mussels, clams, red snapper, rockfish, tuna, and wahoo stand out on Bermudian menus. Bermuda's agricultural history, especially its famous crop of Bermuda onions, also influences cuisine. Today, other seasonal fruits and vegetables grown on the islands include potatoes, carrots, leeks, tomatoes, corn, broccoli, strawberries, cherries, bananas, and loquats.

AN INTERNATIONAL MIX

Perhaps the most unique thing about the food in Bermuda is that very little of it is actually from Bermuda. About 80 percent of the food put on families' tables or sold in restaurants is imported, usually from the United States. The lobsters served during the fall and winter months are caught in Bermuda's waters, but the rest of the time they come from Maine or Canada. For plants grown on the island, chances are their seeds

"The onion is the pride and joy of Bermuda. It is her jewel, her gem of gems. In her conversation, her pulpit, her literature, it is her most frequent and eloquent figure."
—Mark Twain

Most Bermudians follow a family recipe to prepare and serve cassava pie on special occasions.

were originally imported. Since most food is imported, grocery shopping and eating out at Bermuda's restaurants can be very expensive.

A variety of Bermudian flavors and recipes are classics on the island. They reflect a combination of English heritage, Portuguese influences, and a touch of the Caribbean. For example, the classic English hot cross buns have been welcomed to the island with a uniquely Bermudian fish-sandwich spin. Red bean soup has been enthusiastically adopted from Bermuda's Portuguese heritage, along with spicy chourico sausage, a stew called *cozido*, and an egg bread named *massa cevada*. Johnny cakes, corn cakes cooked on the griddle, show the influence of the Caribbean and the Native American roots of many Bermudians. International influences combined with local ingredients and traditions have resulted in a host of popular Bermudian dishes. The ingredients may be imported, but the way they are prepared makes them uniquely Bermudian.

FAVORITE DISHES

One of the most common dishes in Bermuda is cassava pie. It dates all the way back to 1612 when settlers first came to the island. They planted the cassava with its long roots. It was dug up, crushed into powder, and used for flour. Today, it is still the basis for making pie, but now the cassava is imported. There are many variations, but the pie usually includes more than a dozen eggs, an entire chicken, 2 pounds (0.9 kilograms) of sugar, 2 pounds (0.9 kg) of pork, and 10 pounds (4.5 kg) of cassava flour. Cassava pie is traditionally eaten for Christmas dinner and served with chow chow, a pickled relish in mustard sauce.

Local cherries are found on the island and are often turned into everything from jams and pies to wine and sherbets. These Surinam cherries look like miniature pumpkins and grow on a number of hedges throughout Bermuda. Add some rum and ice cream, and you have flaming Surinam cherries!

Parts of the Good Friday and Easter holidays in Bermuda involve several special recipes. Hot cross buns, a decidedly English dessert, are popular. They are found in bakeries or made at home. These square sticky buns have white icing added to their tops in the shape of a cross.

Another holiday favorite is codfish cakes. They are made from salted cod mashed with cooked potatoes and fresh herbs like parsley and thyme. This mixture is formed into patties, dredged in flour, and then pan-fried before being served. Codfish cakes can be eaten with bananas and served for breakfast or sandwiched inside a hot cross bun for a unique Bermudian treat on Good Friday and Easter Sunday. Often, the salted codfish has to be imported from Canada in time for these celebrations.

On Guy Fawkes Day, November 5, sweet potato pudding is popular. Sweet potatoes are baked into a casserole of sugar, butter, milk, and warming spices. Other sweet potato recipes are served throughout the fall.

The national dish in Bermuda is fish chowder. It was introduced by the first colonists. It starts with a stock made from local fish—tails and heads included. Other ingredients include water, bacon fat, salt, tomatoes, cloves, and potatoes. It is simmered slowly for several hours. The chowder is traditionally served with a splash of black rum and a dash of sherry peppers sauce, a kind of hot sauce.

Fresh, locally caught fish is often grilled or fried. Some fish dishes include shark fritters, shark hash, and baked red snapper. Wahoo is a popular fresh catch in Bermuda. It is commonly put in salads along with carrots, ginger, cranberries, vinegar, and soy sauce.

Bean soups are familiar dishes. One version features black-eyed peas. Another type of bean soup is made from red beans, based on a spicy recipe from the Portuguese. This is commonly served as an appetizer.

Fish chowder can be traced back to Bermuda's first colonists. Its spiciness sets it apart from other similar soups.

Codfish probably rose to popularity when Bermudian salt traders swapped their goods for salted cod in Newfoundland.

Sunday breakfast or brunch is a favorite mealtime in Bermuda. The most traditional Sunday morning plate is filled with boiled, salted codfish and boiled potatoes. Bacon, onions, and tomato sauce are added, then topped off with a hard-boiled egg and slices of banana and avocado.

Thanks to its links with England, afternoon tea is another tradition in Bermuda. Whether for locals at home or tourists at hotels, tea is often served between 3 p.m. and 5 p.m. Silver, fine china, and linens introduce a sense of formality. Commonly, the hot tea is accompanied by finger sandwiches with thinly sliced cucumbers. Scones covered in strawberry jam add a sweet touch.

Salted codfish, boiled potatoes, sliced bananas, and various toppings make for a filling Sunday breakfast.

An unusual yellow-orange, plumlike fruit called the loquat is popular on the islands as well. It grows on trees and is tart but tasty. It is made into jams and relishes. Local people eat this fruit right off the tree or turn it into drinks.

Other favorites include Hoppin' John or Peas 'n' Rice, a meal that originally came for the Carolinas. It is made out of rice cooked with beans or black-eyed peas. Johnny cakes served with peas and rice are commonly eaten for breakfast. Their name may have come from a Native American word, or it could be related to their suitability as a food to pack for journeys.

Considering Bermuda's history, it is not surprising that a lot of dishes made on the island use onions. Recipes for onion casseroles, onion bread, onion soup, onion pie, and onion soufflé have been passed down. Bermuda onions are also eaten raw in salads or sandwiches. Locally grown Bermuda onions can be purchased at farm stands and markets in the spring.

More recent additions to the Bermudian repertoire include yeast popcorn and fish sandwiches. Popcorn seasoned with nutritional yeast is a favorite snack that can be made at home or bought packaged. Fish sandwiches from Art Mel's Spicy Dicy restaurant have become famous among locals and tourists. The salty-sweet creation is made with battered and fried fish sandwiched between raisin bread and overloaded with coleslaw, lettuce, tomato, and tartar sauce.

Many drinks are based on Bermuda's favorite Gosling's Black Seal Rum or mixed with the local Barritt's Ginger Beer. Both Gosling's and Barritt's have operated on the island since the 1800s. Local wines are made from Bermuda mulberries and Surinam cherries.

Desserts on the island are usually fruity. They incorporate bananas, loquats, cherries, and tropical fruits. Another common ingredient is rum, which turns up in a variety of cakes.

Bermuda honey is a favorite sweetener. Bees were brought to the island in 1624.

INTERNET LINKS

outerbridge.com/op/sherry-peppers
Visit this website to learn the origin story of one of Bermuda's most famous condiments and favorite addition to fish chowder: Outerbridge's sherry peppers.

www.gotobermuda.com
Bermuda's official travel website offers a visitor's guide to the best food and restaurants in Bermuda.

www.thebermudian.com
The Bermudian is an online magazine with a wide variety of classic Bermudian recipes to try, including codfish cakes, fish chowder, onion pie, and savory onion bread.

JOHNNY CAKES

1 cup (128 grams) cornmeal
1 cup (128 g) all-purpose flour
¼ cup (32 g) sugar
½ teaspoon salt
1 teaspoon baking soda
¾ cup (177 milliliters) buttermilk
oil or butter for the pan

Place cornmeal, flour, sugar, salt, and baking soda in a large bowl, and stir with a whisk to fully combine.

Add the buttermilk to the dry mixture using a wooden spoon. With your hands, form the batter into six equal-sized balls.

On a floured surface, flatten each ball until it is about 1 inch (2.54 cm) thick.

Heat butter or oil in a skillet over medium-high heat. Add the johnny cakes to the skillet, and cook about 3 minutes on each side, until the cakes are slightly puffed and golden brown in color.

YEAST POPCORN

⅓ cup (43 g) popcorn kernels
2 tablespoons coconut oil or
    canola oil
2—3 tablespoons nutritional yeast
sea salt to taste
sprinkle of sugar (optional)

Measure the oil into a medium lidded saucepan, and set over medium-high heat.

Add three popcorn kernels to the oil. Once the kernels pop, add the remaining popcorn to the pan, and cover with the lid.

Shake the pan about every 15 seconds to keep the popcorn from burning. When the popping slows down, remove the pan from the heat, and pour the popcorn into a large bowl.

Add the nutritional yeast, sea salt, and optional sugar to the bowl of popcorn. Use your hands to evenly coat the popcorn in the seasonings.

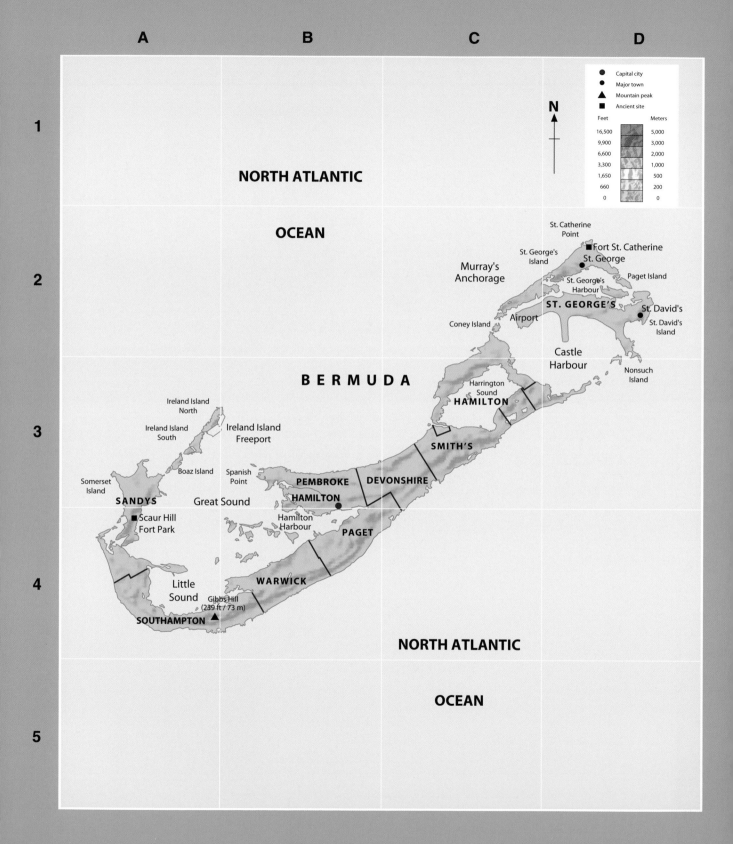

A B C D

1

NORTH ATLANTIC

OCEAN

2

St. Catherine
Point

■ Fort St. Catherine
● St. George

Murray's
Anchorage

St. George's
Island

Paget Island

St. George's
Harbour

ST. GEORGE'S

Coney Island

Airport

● St. David's

St. David's
Island

Castle
Harbour

Nonsuch
Island

BERMUDA

Harrington
Sound

HAMILTON

3

Ireland Island
North

Ireland Island
South

Ireland Island
Freeport

SMITH'S

Somerset
Island

Boaz Island

Spanish
Point

PEMBROKE

DEVONSHIRE

SANDYS

Great Sound

HAMILTON ●

■ Scaur Hill
Fort Park

Hamilton
Harbour

PAGET

4

Little
Sound

WARWICK

Gibbs Hill
(239 ft / 73 m)

SOUTHAMPTON ▲

NORTH ATLANTIC

OCEAN

5

● Capital city
● Major town
▲ Mountain peak
■ Ancient site

N

Feet   Meters
16,500   5,000
9,900   3,000
6,600   2,000
3,300   1,000
1,650   500
660   200
0   0

MAP OF BERMUDA

ECONOMIC BERMUDA

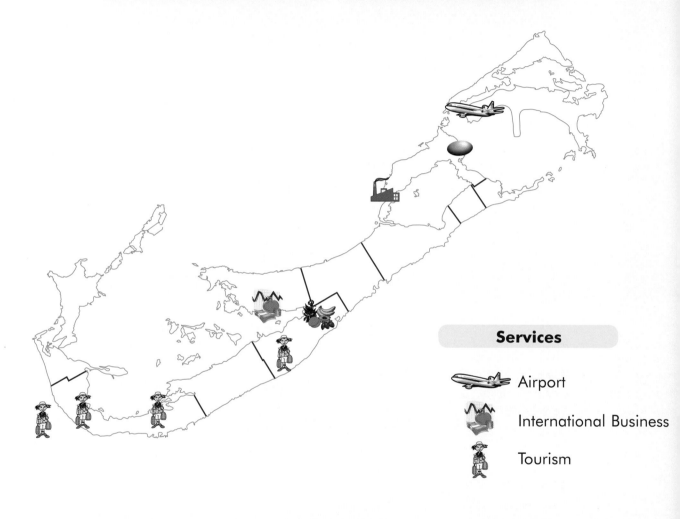

Services

✈ Airport

International Business

🧍 Tourism

Agriculture

 Bananas, onions, citrus fruits, and flowers

Manufacturing

🏭 Food, beverages, carpentry, wood, and publishing

Natural Resources

⬮ Limestone

ABOUT THE ECONOMY

All figures are 2016 estimates unless otherwise noted.

OVERVIEW
Bermuda has one of the highest per capita incomes in the world, primarily based on tourism and international business; its industrial sector is small; and agriculture is limited.

POPULATION
63,908 (2019)

LAND AREA
21 square miles (54 sq km)

POVERTY RATE
11 percent (2008)

AGRICULTURAL PRODUCTS
semitropical produce, dairy products, flowers, honey

CURRENCY
Bermuda dollar

GROSS DOMESTIC PRODUCT
$7.48 billion (2019)

GDP BY SECTORS
agriculture: 0.9 percent; industry: 5.3 percent; services: 93.8 percent

MAIN IMPORTS
pharmaceuticals, food, alcohol, automobiles

MAIN EXPORTS
structural concrete products, paints, perfumes, furniture

MAJOR TRADE PARTNERS
exports: Jamaica, Luxembourg, United States; imports: United States, South Korea, Canada

PORTS AND HARBORS
Hamilton and St. George's

CULTURAL BERMUDA

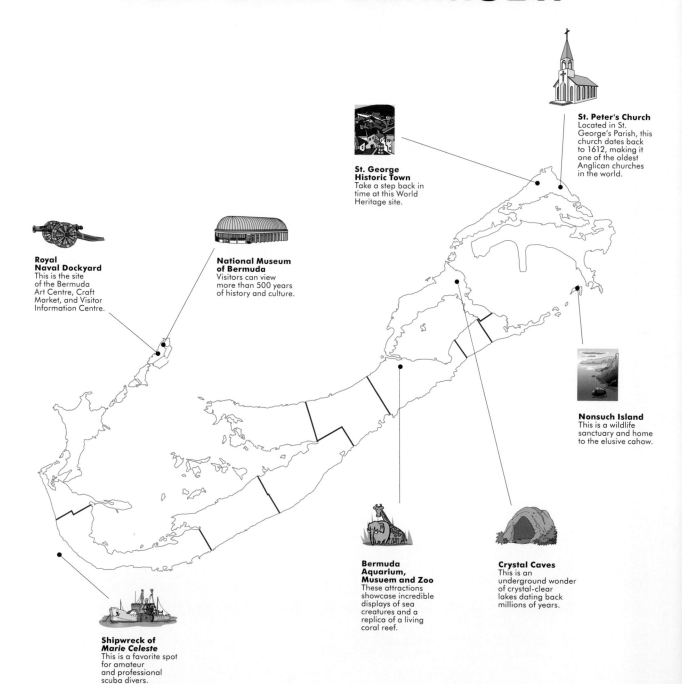

St. Peter's Church
Located in St. George's Parish, this church dates back to 1612, making it one of the oldest Anglican churches in the world.

St. George Historic Town
Take a step back in time at this World Heritage site.

Royal Naval Dockyard
This is the site of the Bermuda Art Centre, Craft Market, and Visitor Information Centre.

National Museum of Bermuda
Visitors can view more than 500 years of history and culture.

Nonsuch Island
This is a wildlife sanctuary and home to the elusive cahow.

Bermuda Aquarium, Musuem and Zoo
These attractions showcase incredible displays of sea creatures and a replica of a living coral reef.

Crystal Caves
This is an underground wonder of crystal-clear lakes dating back millions of years.

Shipwreck of Marie Celeste
This is a favorite spot for amateur and professional scuba divers.

ABOUT THE CULTURE

All figures are 2016 estimates unless otherwise noted.

OFFICIAL NAME
Bermuda

CAPITAL
City of Hamilton

NATIONAL FLAG
red, with the flag of the United Kingdom on the inner half and the Bermudian coat of arms portraying the sinking of the *Sea Venture* centered on the outer half

NATIONAL ANTHEM
"Hail to Bermuda" (unofficial), "God Save the Queen" (official)

PARISHES
Devonshire, Hamilton, Paget, Pembroke, Sandys, Smith's, Southampton, St. George's, and Warwick

ETHNIC GROUPS
Black 52 percent, white 31 percent, mixed race 9 percent, Asian 4 percent, other 4 percent

MAJOR RELIGIONS
Protestant 46.2 percent (including Anglican 15.8 percent, African Methodist Episcopal 8.6 percent, Seventh-day Adventist 6.7 percent), Roman Catholic 14.5 percent, other Christian 9 percent, Muslim 1 percent, Jewish 1 percent, none 17.8 percent (2010)

LIFE EXPECTANCY
81 years (2019)

LITERACY
98 percent

HOLIDAYS AND FESTIVALS
New Year's Day (January 1), Good Friday (March or April), Easter (March or April), Queen Elizabeth II's birthday (June 11), Emancipation Day/Somers Day/Cup Match (August), Remembrance Day (November 11), Christmas Day (December 25), Boxing Day (December 26)

TIMELINE

IN BERMUDA	IN THE WORLD
	1492 Christopher Columbus sails to the Caribbean.
1503 Juan de Bermúdez sights the island.	**1530** The beginning of transatlantic slave trade is organized by the Portuguese in Africa.
1609 Admiral Sir George Somers shipwrecks on the island in the *Sea Venture*.	
1610 The *Deliverance* and *Patience* set sail for Jamestown.	
1612 The Virginia Company sends 60 settlers to Bermuda to establish a colony.	
1616 The first enslaved people are brought to Bermuda.	
1620 Bermuda's first parliament meets at St. Peter's Church.	**1620** Pilgrims sail the *Mayflower* to America.
1684 Bermuda becomes a British colony.	
	1776 The U.S. Declaration of Independence is written.
1810 The Royal Naval Dockyard is built.	**1789–1799** The French Revolution occurs.
1815 The capital is moved from St. George's to Hamilton.	
1834 Slavery is abolished in Great Britain and its territories.	**1861** The American Civil War begins.
	1869 The Suez Canal is opened.
1883 Princess Louise visits Bermuda, starting the tourism business.	**1914** World War I begins.
1941 The United States leases a part of the island.	**1939** World War II begins.

IN BERMUDA	IN THE WORLD
1944	
Women are given the vote for the first time.	**1945**
	The United States drops atomic bombs on Hiroshima and Nagasaki.
	1957
1959	The Russians launch *Sputnik 1*.
The Theatre Boycott leads to desegregation.	
1963	
The Progressive Labour Party is formed.	
1964	
The United Bermuda Party is formed.	**1966–1969**
1968	The Chinese Cultural Revolution takes place.
A new constitution is introduced, and the first election is held.	
1971	
Schools are desegregated.	
1973	
Governor Richard Sharples is assassinated.	
	1991
	The breakup of the Soviet Union occurs.
	1997
2000	Hong Kong is returned to China.
St. George becomes a UNESCO World Heritage site.	**2001**
	Terrorists crash planes in New York; Washington, D.C.; and Pennsylvania on September 11.
2003	**2003**
Hurricane Fabian damages the island.	The Iraq War begins.
2004	
There is not enough public support for independence from the United Kingdom.	**2008**
	Barack Obama is elected the first African American president of the United States.
2009	
Queen Elizabeth II visits Bermuda.	
2014	
Hurricane Fay and Hurricane Gonzalo cause damage.	**2015**
	Over 80 nations sign the Paris Climate Agreement.
2020	**2020**
The COVID-19 pandemic hits Bermuda.	The United Kingdom withdraws from the European Union (Brexit).

GLOSSARY

abolition
Bringing slavery to an end.

archipelago
A large group or chain of islands.

aristocrat
A person with the taste, manners, and background of wealth.

blockade
Cutting off an area with troops or warships to prevent people or supplies from coming or going.

decode
To break or decipher a code.

emancipation
The act of releasing or freeing someone from bondage or control.

equity
Fairness or justice.

espionage
The act or practice of spying.

islet
A very small island.

microorganism
An organism too small to see with the unaided eye.

parish
A subdivision of land.

parliamentary democracy
A system of government where people elect representatives to parliament to make laws.

pharmaceutical
Relating to pharmacy or drugs for medical treatment.

potable
Suitable for drinking.

quarry
An above-ground excavation site of building stone or slate.

regalia
Decorations, insignia, or ceremonial clothes of an office.

schooner
A sailing vessel having at least two masts.

segregate
To separate or set apart from others; to require a separation.

sloop
A sailing vessel with a single mast about one-third of the boat's length.

suffrage
The right to vote.

tier
One of a series of layers.

FOR FURTHER INFORMATION

BOOKS

Bardgett, Robyn, and Melissa Fox. *Fodor's Bermuda*. New York, NY: Fodor's Travel, 2020.

Gehrman, Elizabeth. *Rare Birds: The Extraordinary Tale of the Bermuda Peterel and the Man Who Brought It Back from Extinction*. Boston, MA: Beacon Press, 2012.

Jones, Rosemary. *Bermuda: Five Centuries*. Bermuda: Panatel VDS, Ltd., 2004.

Karwoski, Gail. *Miracle: The True Story of the Wreck of the Sea Venture.* Plain City, OH: Darby Creek Publishing, 2004.

Stine, Megan. *Where Is the Bermuda Triangle?* New York, NY: Penguin Workshop, 2018.

Webbe, Florenz Maxwell. *Girlcott*. Kingston, Jamaica: Blouse & Skirt Books, 2017.

WEBSITES

Bermuda National Trust. www.bnt.bm.

Bermuda Tourism Authority. www.gotobermuda.com.

The Bermudian. www.thebermudian.com.

CIA. *The World Fact Book*. "Bermuda." www.cia.gov/the-world-factbook/countries/bermuda.

Government of Bermuda. www.gov.bm.

BIBLIOGRAPHY

Bardgett, Robyn, and Melissa Fox. *Fodor's Bermuda*. New York, NY: Fodor's Travel, 2020.

Bermuda Audobon Society. https://www.audubon.bm.

"Bermuda History and Heritage." *Smithsonian Magazine*, November 6, 2007. www.smithsonianmag.com/travel/bermuda-history-and-heritage-14340790.

Bermuda National Trust. "Black History in Bermuda: Teacher Resource Guide." https://www.bnt.bm/images/News%20Articles/Black%20History%20Book.pdf.

Bermuda National Trust. "Spittal Pond Nature Reserve: Teacher Resource Guide." https://www.bnt.bm/images/documents/spittal_pond.pdf.

Bermuda Tourism Authority. www.gotobermuda.com.

The Bermudian. www.thebermudian.com.

CIA. *The World Fact Book*. "Bermuda." www.cia.gov/the-world-factbook/countries/bermuda.

Dash, Mike. "White Gold: How Salt Made the Turks and Caicos Islands." *Smithsonian Magazine*, December 4, 2012. https://www.smithsonianmag.com/history/white-gold-how-salt-made-and-unmade-the-turks-and-caicos-islands-161576195/.

Department of Culture, Bermuda. www.communityandculture.bm.

Encyclopedia Britannica. "Bermuda." www.britannica.com/place/Bermuda.

Gehrman, Elizabeth. *Rare Birds: The Extraordinary Tale of the Bermuda Peterel and the Man Who Brought It Back from Extinction*. Boston, MA: Beacon Press, 2012.

Government of Bermuda. www.gov.bm.

Government of Bermuda, Department of Statistics. www.gov.bm/department/statistics.

Hoffman, Donald. *Mark Twain in Paradise: His Voyages to Bermuda*. Columbia, MO: University of Missouri Press, 2006.

Jones, Rosemary. *Bermuda: Five Centuries*. Bermuda: Panatel VDS, Ltd., 2004.

Prince, Mary. *The History of Mary Prince, A West Indian Slave, Related by Herself*. Edited by Moira Ferguson. London, UK: Pandora Press, 1987.

Swan, Quito. *Black Power in Bermuda: The Struggle for Decolonization*. New York, NY: Palgrave Macmillan, 2009.

World Wildlife Fund: Bermuda. www.worldwildlife.org/ecoregions/na0301.

INDEX

INDEX